Shelter from the Storm

Shelter from the Storm

Caring for a Child with a Life-Threatening Condition

Joanne M. Hilden, M.D.
and Daniel R. Tobin, M.D.
with Karen Lindsey

PERSEUS
PUBLISHING

A Member of the Perseus Books Group

A Life Institute Book

Library of Congress Control Number: 2002114134
ISBN 0–7382-0534–6

Perseus Publishing is a member of the Perseus Books Group.
Find us on the World Wide Web at http://www.perseuspublishing.com.

Perseus Publishing books are available at special discounts for bulk purchases in the U.S. by corporations, institutions, and other organizations. For more information, please contact the Special Markets Department at the Perseus Books Group, 11 Cambridge Center, Cambridge, MA 02142, or call (800) 255-1514 or (617) 252-5298, or e-mail j.mccrary@perseusbooks.com.

Text design by the Perseus Books Group
Set in 12-point Minion by the Perseus Books Group

First printing, January 2003

2 3 4 5 6 7 8 9 10—06 05 04 03

To our children, David and Kelly Hilden
and Brian and Jeremy Tobin, whose health and
joyful days we appreciate with all our beings.

Thank you, God, for the wonderful life I have had so far.

Christian Olaf Osen
1990–1999

CONTENTS

A NOTE ON LANGUAGE

*W*riting about any group of people can become awkward when there is need to refer to hypothetical individuals among them. Do we assume that all of them are male, though they clearly are not, and risk offending some readers by using a universal "he"? Or do we choose instead to use the more accurate, but extremely awkward, "he or she"? Many writers, most notably the famous child specialist Dr. Benjamin Spock, have chosen a third option: In each chapter, the hypothetical individual is represented by one gender, to be followed in the next chapter by the other gender. If "the child" is "he" in Chapter 1, Chapter 2 will refer to "she," and so forth. We feel this is the alternative that best combines accuracy and grace of language, and so have chosen it.

This book has two authors. Dr. Joanne Hilden's major work is with severely ill children and their parents. Dr. Daniel Tobin wrote the book *Peaceful Dying*, which provides the concepts we have adopted to the specific population of children with life-threatening illnesses, and to their families. Unless otherwise specified, the "I" referred to will always be Dr. Hilden. Stories about children and their families reflect the experience of not only Dr. Hilden, but of her many colleagues around the country as well.

Finally, we have changed the names of patients and their families to protect their privacy.

FOREWORD

We are two parents who had to struggle with our children's life-threatening illnesses. At the age of 3, Nancy's daughter Kathryn was stricken with high-risk acute lymphoblastic leukemia. Winnie's son Eric developed osteosarcoma (a bone tumor) at age 15.

Nancy's story: Treatment for Kathryn's life-threatening disease was very difficult. It threw the family into turmoil that we had never before experienced. My way to cope was to research all treatment and supportive care options and to advocate for the very best for Kathryn. One area that was difficult but necessary to explore was appropriate end-of-life care.

I made many friends in the new community of childhood cancer, just as parents with children who have other life-threatening diseases do. Some of the children I met lived; and sadly, some died. But even sadder to my family was the distancing of medical personnel and the inadequacy of pain control available at the end of many children's lives. Other families were able to create a loving and humane end of life for their children. Watching how other families coped encouraged me to fully explore the limited resources available to families about end-of-life comfort care. It made me feel more prepared intellectually and emotionally to think about these heart-rending issues early rather than later.

Thankfully, I did not need to use the information I learned about end-of-life care. Kathryn survived her lengthy and difficult treatments. She is now a 14-year-old who ice-skates and loves to read. I am grateful that she is still with us and happy that I prepared for all possibilities.

Winnie's story: I wasn't as lucky as Nancy; my son Eric died at age 17 surrounded by his family. After he had completed his initial treatment, I had every reason to believe that he would survive. When he relapsed just six months later, I was crushed. He had surgery to remove metastatic tumors, and I still had hope for a cure. When the tumors returned, our family decided on surgery again as the best option. Our doctor told us, "If I tell you we need to do more chemo, I will be giving you bad news."

That was the first indication that Eric's chance for cure was growing smaller. When his tumors returned yet again, his doctor said that surgery was no longer an option and chemotherapy would buy time. Although it was unspoken, all were hoping that Eric would live for at least three months. Because of that hope, their positive attitude, and diligent medical and nursing care, we were blessed with ten months.

If I had been given a choice, Eric would have been cured. When I realized that cure was unlikely, I knew that I wanted to prepare as best as I possibly could. I had prepared for the birth of Eric, my firstborn child, with great care. I decided to count it a privilege to be able to prepare for his death.

We are both so sorry that you are grappling with the fear that your child may die. It's something we didn't expect when we became parents. But just as we wish the best for our children in life, we try to do the best for our children in death. We each have to evaluate the treatments available and balance the risks and benefits of what has been proposed. We each think about how we will manage if the treatments are not successful. We need to face these choices as a family.

Regardless of what illness or trauma threatens the life of your child, coping is very difficult in the beginning. After the terror, the denial, and the guilt, most parents of seriously ill children begin to walk forward with hope. Treating serious illness in children has been one of modern medicine's success stories. The cure rates for many childhood diseases (especially childhood cancer) have dramatically risen in the last three decades. There is good reason for hope.

This book talks about taking care of yourself and your other children; how to learn to live day by day, and, when necessary, hour by hour. It helps you think about the hard choices: How to consider new treatments and yet prepare for the end. It can help you, when necessary, to redefine hope: shifting from hope for a cure, to hope for more time, to hope for a loving, peaceful, and pain-free death. It takes your hand and guides you down a path you don't want to walk. But we sometimes must trudge forward because we don't have a choice. As Abraham Lincoln said, "I may walk slowly, but I don't walk backward."

This book will help you look inside yourself and find the best way for your family to keep walking forward. It can help you choose the best treatments while preparing for the possibility that they might not work. And, it can help you find peace if the time comes to stop treating the disease. It gives clear advice so you can make sure that your child's pain is managed well and that communication is open and ongoing. It helps you create a strong partnership with the medical team, so that they can support your family's choices and make the journey easier. It can make the difference between grief complicated by anger, rage, or guilt, and grief that flows from a peaceful, loving end.

This book will also help you discuss choices with your children. Most children need to talk with their friends, families, and siblings about their end-of-life journey. Many give away prized possessions, write good-bye letters, and enjoy visits from those who love them. If allowed, children and teens do a very good job of wrapping up their loose ends. They are often visited in their dreams by grandparents and friends who have died. Talking about these plans and dreams brings many families closer together. It helps them create their own way to face and walk this part of the journey.

As parents, we are supported by our friends and community. It will be especially helpful for them to read this book as well. By knowing what you are facing, they will be able to support you in a more thoughtful and helpful manner.

When we learned of our children's illnesses, each of us searched the literature for books or articles to help us begin to think about the possibility of death, but found little that could help. We both would have learned much had this book been available when we were walking that difficult path.

We encourage you to read this book with an open mind. Regard it as a type of insurance policy—something that you wouldn't be without, but hope never to use. Realize that each member of your family, and indeed even your friends, will set their own pace. With help and guidance you will begin to equip yourself to meet whatever challenges you face.

Best wishes for a smooth and peaceful journey.

Winnie Kittiko, R.N., M.S.
Eric's mom
Clinical Educator
AFLAC Cancer Center and Blood Disorders Service
Children's Healthcare of Atlanta at Scottish Rite
Member—Children's Oncology Group End-of-Life
Care Committee

Nancy Keene
Kathryn's mom
Author of *Childhood Leukemia, Childhood Cancer, Childhood Cancer Survivors, Working with Your Doctor, Your Child in the Hospital,* and *Chemo, Craziness, and Comfort: Your Book About Cancer*

Preface

*E*arly in 1998, a friend introduced me to Dr. Joanne Hilden. Joanne was a pediatric oncologist with a passionate interest in improving the field of pediatric palliative care, both locally and nationally. I was immediately struck by Joanne's profound commitment to creating new tools and medical models that would help children, as well as their parents, face potential end-of-life situations. It was clear to me that her colleagues in pediatric medicine, like mine in adult medicine, were just beginning to address the unique psychological, spiritual, and physical needs of people facing life-threatening illness.

At our first meeting, Joanne and I concluded that we could contribute to pediatric medicine by creating a model of structured conversations that would help physicians and parents communicate. I had already created such a model, Advanced Illness Coordinated Care (AICC), to help adults cope with advanced illness. I hoped that Joanne and I might create a similar model focused on the needs of the pediatric population and their families. Joanne incorporated her experience and insight from her clinical practice and compassionately and thoroughly created a model for conversations that would help parents gather information and guidance when facing their child's life-threatening illness.

Since the time we met, I have watched with great admiration as Joanne has become a national leader in pediatric oncology and pediatric palliative care. It is my sincere hope that the communication model we created in this book, which has been developed into the Pediatric Advanced Illness Coordinated Care (PAICC) Program, will continue to grow and be integrated into routine medical care. It is a great honor for me to contribute to the work that I am confident will ease the suffering of many children and their parents as they face what is surely the most painful and difficult experience of their lives.

Daniel R. Tobin, M.D.

Introduction:
Why This Book?

*I*f you're reading this book, it's probably been recommended by a family member, doctor, nurse, or social worker because your child has a life-threatening illness or injury. In the midst of this storm, with all your heart and soul, you hope for your child's recovery. But you know, either in your own heart or in the words of the people who suggested this book, that there is a chance that he won't recover. And as you continue to do all that you can for his cure, you may realize that you need to prepare for the other possibility, painful as it may be.

This book has been written from a desire to help and comfort you, but with the knowledge that we as writers cannot really know what you're going through. For this reason, we looked to other parents to help us to understand the many needs that come up. So perhaps as you read the difficult parts, it might help you to know that the advice comes from people who have walked in your shoes and emerged with a desire to help others.

A child with a serious illness or injury often spends considerable time in the hospital or in specialists' offices. Doctors and nurses join his parents in a very intensive fight to keep the child alive. It can take days or weeks; indeed, it sometimes takes months and even years. But eventually, most of these children make it. To see your child survive and continue to grow is one of the most rewarding experiences in the world, however uncertain and even hellishly painful the times leading up to the clean bill of health have been. Life then goes on, more precious than before. The child graduates from high school or college, maybe gets married and has children of his own. Often parents have sent graduation announcements and wedding pictures back to the doctors and nurses who cared for their child. These pictures and announcements are hung on the walls in our hospitals and clinics; go to any oncology clinic or heart disease clinic and you'll find them. They keep the doctors and nurses going.

Sadly, it doesn't always work out this way. In spite of our best efforts, in spite of the hard work and prayers of the parents and loved ones, the child sometimes dies. When it becomes clear that he is dying—and this may be at the beginning of the illness or injury, or months later—parents need further and different medical information in order to prepare for what is ahead, and to make decisions with the doctors as best they can. The doctors and nurses cannot always predict which children are going to survive and which are going to die. They try their best to predict this; they want to be honest with people. But some very sick children have gotten better, while some children who seemed much less ill have died. In my years of working with children, I have found it helpful to provide parents with information about what to expect if their child gets sicker, just in case.

If the information turns out to be unnecessary, I rejoice with the parents at its uselessness. But too often, I have seen situations in which the turning point has been missed, or has been too swift. The only thing more horrible for parents than the loss of a child is the *unexpected* loss of a child: So much is left undone; the child has undergone suffering that he might have been spared; parents anguish at not having been prepared.

The purpose of this book, then, is this: To help all parents dealing with the life-threatening condition of a child. It's always a horribly difficult time, whatever the outcome—the child's suffering and helplessness, the uncertainty, the hopes, the fears. This book is created to help you to feel some guidance in the dark, to help you make all the decisions you will need to make during this time.

As you begin to take in the gravity of your child's condition, please know this: If your child has to die, he can die peacefully. You can make sure he is free of pain. You can make sure that everyone has a chance to say good-bye, and above all to say "I love you." You can get the help that you and your family need to get through this, and to make sure your child's death is peaceful. This book is designed to help you do that.

You may not want to consider the prospect at all. It can be too painful, and it can seem as if the very fact of looking at the possibility of your child's death somehow makes it more likely. But it doesn't. Preparing for the possible death of your child does not make it happen, nor does it make death come faster than it otherwise would have. It does not mean that you are giving up. Helping yourself and your family to prepare for something that never happens does not harm you; it can actually strengthen you. And it can do this even if your child survives. Facing the worst scenario is never wasted effort in this kind of situation. Whatever the outcome, looking at all the scenarios gives you more control of the situation and enables you to make medical decisions for your child.

Shelter from the Storm: Caring for a Child with a Life-Threatening Condition has been developed to help you to cope with whatever happens throughout the course of your child's illness. Our goal is to empower you to fight for your child's life as long as recovery is a reasonable expectation, while at the same time preparing you to deal with the process of his dying, if that turns out to be inevitable. Your child can have a peaceful death, and you can learn to achieve whatever peace of mind is possible in such a shattering situation.

Peaceful dying can be very hard to arrange. Sometimes health care providers lack the training and perspective to offer patients a physically and emotionally comfortable end to their lives. There are many medical, societal, and economic barriers to excellent end-of-life care. My coauthor, Dr. Dan Tobin, recognized these obstacles and wrote *Peaceful Dying: The Step-by-Step Guide to Preserving Your Dignity, Your Choice, and Your Inner Peace at the End of Life.* This book addresses the adult patient and, secondarily, his loved ones. It gives people facing such situations a list of practical instructions (arranged in an A–Z fashion) for this difficult time. It empowers patients and their families to ask for and obtain the help they need, and it helps them to deal with the emotional and spiritual issues that arise.

But the situation of a dying child is special. For one thing, children and adolescents don't make most of their own decisions. Parents of children with advanced illness have to make tough choices at an emotional time. Teens and mature pre-adolescents can participate in the process, but parents of a very young or incapacitated child must essentially make all his decisions for him. This can be incredibly difficult for a parent: Our goal is to help you learn how to make the decisions that are right for you and your child.

Sick children are still growing, which is a biological process very much like healing. So when a child is diagnosed with an illness such as cancer or heart disease, for example, he is much more likely to be cured than is an adult. That possibility of cure is a wonderful thing, but it can make the process of dealing with a child's illness unpredictable. These children sometimes have several medical crises in which the doctor thinks they might die. How is a parent to know if the child will or won't pull through this time? Each crisis means facing the child's mortality once again; each recovery means another chance at life, perhaps at permanent cure.

Further, parents simply do not expect to outlive their children. We expect to die in old age as our children are in the midst of their own, healthy middle age. Most of the time, we are correct in our expectations. The death of a child is a rare event in developed nations nowadays. The logical expectation of longevity, combined with our society's overall tendency to deny the reality of death, makes it almost impossible to believe that one's own child is dying. In *Shelter from the Storm* we present the concepts introduced to adults in *Peaceful Dying* as they apply to children. We offer a philosophy and an approach that acknowledge the special difficulty parents have in preparing for the loss of a child. And we help you to help your child to die peacefully, in case death is inevitable.

The difficulty that doctors have in predicting whether a particular child will live or die, and the difficulty that families have in accepting a terminal prognosis, can often result in delaying referral to hospice services, or to what we call "palliative care" services (which we explain in Step H). Such care need not be confined to the dying: It can and should be available to anyone who is seriously ill.

Perhaps as you read this you are facing your child's death in the next few days or weeks. Children die from injuries sustained in car crashes, for example, sometimes spending just hours or days in intensive care units first. Or maybe what will happen to your child is unclear. Infants may die from premature birth, and often the family goes through a time involving ventilators and very high technology medicine. Cancer, heart disease, and cystic fibrosis are among the most common medical causes of death in childhood, and the process of dying from such illnesses can be a long one. There are also rare conditions (for example, of the brain or lungs) that create progressive deterioration; the child and his family endure the slow worsening and unpredictable time course. While these situations differ, there is a common need for information and preparation. Whatever the situation, there is help for you in this book.

We wrote this to help families dealing with many different life-threatening childhood illnesses and injuries, which may or may not result in the child's death. Many children with serious illnesses or injuries recover, but at the beginning, their chances of recovery are unclear. *Not all parts of the book will apply to every child.* If you wish, skip over the background discussions and start at Chapter 2, where our "steps" begin.

As you go through it, parts of the book may make you angry, and many will make you sad. Some parts may surprise you. There are sections you may not be ready for, and you can save them to read at a later time. Because we understand and expect that different sections will be helpful to different readers at various phases of their experience, we restate certain facts throughout the book. Thus you will find key ideas in whichever section of the book you find useful at whatever times in your child's condition you are reading them. We have written the text as "steps" not to imply that things happen in a fixed order but for organizational purposes. We realize that some of the steps will be relevant all the time and some only at certain times. Consider the steps to be areas you can go to as needed, depending on what happens with your child and on what your own needs demand.

You and your entire family can try to prepare for your child's possible death. While it may seem impossible to believe now, you can experience the death as a peaceful process, and you can survive. You may even be able to find meaning in this desolating experience. You can learn from your child and continue to find pride and fulfillment in the knowledge that you are effectively helping him even at the most painful hour. Many parents have told us of these feelings, even in the midst of their grief. Indeed, the input of parents who have gone through a child's serious illness has been an invaluable part of preparing this book.

With their natural tendency to live in the present and their ability to cherish play and pleasant experiences, dying children often astound the adults around them. Over and over, they have shown adults how to cope and grow through it, and it becomes an extraordinary privilege for the medical staff to participate in their care. We are changed for the better in caring for your children. It is in the spirit of your child's strength, resilience, and permanent place in the hearts of your family that we offer you *Shelter from the Storm: Caring for a Child with a Life-Threatening Condition.*

❧

My Journey to This Work

I never doubted that I would specialize in pediatric oncology: I decided on that when I decided to go to medical school. I liked the idea of fighting cancer: It was a smart, formidable foe, clever in a sinister way. It knew how to hide, yet how to grow. I had the kind of hate for it that can inspire and motivate a good doctor on hard days.

I also knew I wanted to work with kids. I saw early in med school how enchanting children were as patients. From the first day I worked with children, they climbed right up into my heart and took up residence. They are engaging as patients; they don't want to talk about being sick. They want to talk about what they're going to do when they get out of your clinic. They want to talk about fun, they want to surprise you, and they want to laugh with you.

I was hooked from the moment one of my mentors, a young pediatric oncologist, took a photograph from her wallet and showed it to me. "Here's one I cured," she said, smiling. The little girl was grinning at the camera, holding up a lollipop. I can still see that picture in detail. I'm willing to bet the doctor still has it. I now have many of my own photos.

During my years in medical school and my residency, this determination only increased. As all residents do, I got deeper and deeper into the battles, saw firsthand how long, complicated, and hard the process was for families faced with a child's serious illness or injury. There is so much to do, so much to understand, and there are so many decisions to make. It became clear that those families who had all the information that they needed were better able than others to deal with what came up. Knowledge, as many parents reminded me, really *is* power.

But in most cases I came to see that information needed to be delivered well in phases. The first phase is the one in which the child and family first entered the medical world—the time right after diagnosis of illness, or right after injury. Parents are in shock, and trying to give them information in a way that they can grasp it is hard. Most of them are asking with their eyes and not with their words, "Will my child die?" Some ask it out loud, but most do not. So I learned how to work with people faced with great uncertainty, who hope for the best but at the same time fear the worst.

Fortunately, most kids do get better, thanks to modern health care. And, as our newspapers tout medical miracles every day, we care for in a world where everyone expects that a child will ultimately emerge from a health crisis with his health intact.

So I learned how to work with children and parents who are facing medical uncertainty in a very optimistic world. I loved working with seriously ill children and teenagers, and the more I experienced this work, the more I was hooked on it. I loved listening to what they had to say; I loved answering their questions. As I worked more and more with such children, I found an added joy in staying in touch with some of them: to see a child I hadn't been sure would make it grow into a healthy adult.

I didn't, of course, always have this opportunity. While most such children survive, some don't. They certainly don't all survive in my specialty of oncology. And I learned how hard it is to lose a child you've worked with, hoped for, and prayed for. I learned too that the parents who had need of a compassionate, involved doctor throughout a child's illness have even more need when it becomes clear that the child will die.

My awakening to the need for programs to help seriously ill and injured children and their parents occurred two weeks into my pediatric residency. I was working in the emergency room when an infant was brought in, suffering cardiac arrest (she was not breathing and had no heartbeat). A rush of doctors and nurses urgently tried to revive her. Several physicians were rapidly preparing intravenous catheters, needles for blood tests, breathing tubes, ventilators, and X-rays. But we soon realized that the baby would not live. "Somebody's got to talk to the parents," a nurse said. She looked at me: I was the only doctor with no needles or tubes in hand. The others glanced up at me briefly and then went back to their work. I had been elected.

I was stunned. I had never done this before: I had no training in how to tell parents their child was dying. Slowly, forcing my body to move, I left the emergency room and walked over to the waiting parents. I saw the fear in their eyes and recognized my own fear. Bumbling, I told them the news. I can't remember what I said; I know it was inadequate. I remember the pain in their faces, and my own mute sympathy. I knew there should be training in how to do this better, that these parents deserved a trained person at this hour. I vowed then to do whatever I could to see that medical school and residency training included teaching doctors how to talk to scared, grieving, and shocked parents.

Throughout the years, I have seen parents bring their children for the best, most specialized medical care in the world, fully expecting them to be cured. It is a natural expectation, and usually it's correct. But some children will not be cured. And when that's the case, parents have the right and the need to know it.

Hearing grim news about their child is hard for parents. Giving them the grim news is hard for doctors. I have seen doctors struggle to force the words out. Sometimes I wondered if there really *was* a good way to tell them.

But then there were the times, tragically few, when the medical team had made the effort, persisted, and succeeded. I saw the difference it made when parents really had been prepared for the eventual death of their child. I saw the powerful compassion and effort it took on the part of doctors, nurses, and their teammates to accomplish that. It made the experience a little less agonizing for the parents, a little more bearable. I believed then, as I do now, that we owe this to parents, and I vowed to be like these doctors. But I didn't want it to be a gamble: If the parents got a sensitive, courageous medical team, good; if not, too bad. I began thinking about how to teach these skills and create programs that would support parents who were going through this agony. I knew then and know now that it is possible to arrange for a child's death to be peaceful.

One of the main differences can be the health care system's approach. I discovered how much better the care is when there is a multidisciplinary medical team (nurse practitioners, nurses, social workers, child life workers, child psychologists, chaplains, and hospice workers) to help the entire family—patient, parents, and siblings. This kind of medicine can be immensely rewarding to practice. "I wouldn't change a thing about my son's death," one parent told me. Repeatedly, my team was thanked for taking time to explain choices to parents, for helping them when they wanted to have their child die at home rather than in the hospital, for encouraging the whole family to come and say good-bye to the dying child. At times they felt empowered by helping their child. "Taking her off the ventilator was the easy part," one father said to me. "It was something I could do for her." A mother who had learned how to control the morphine drip at home was gratified that her daughter was able to play with her brother, since she was in so much less pain than she had been.

As a practicing children's cancer doctor, I joined committees of health care providers, both locally and nationally, whose goals were to improve the care of the dying. Thankfully, working on these committees has connected me with other people seeking solutions. The hospice and the palliative care movements are being led by people who are funding research, bringing end-of-life care issues to medical education, creating legislation, teaching home care providers how to deal with dying children, and creating public education to help patients and their families advocate for what is needed. We hope and believe that, as a result, seriously ill adults and children will receive better pain and symptom control, *regardless of whether or not they are dying.*

But all of that requires actually talking about it—acknowledging the seriousness of your child's condition. As the parents of a seriously ill child, to be of the most help to your child throughout his illness, you will need to be willing to talk about the unthinkable. In my journey through this work, I have learned from the children themselves how much they are helped if their parents are enabled to do that.

❦

TREATING THE LIVING AND CARING FOR THE DYING: WHERE IN THIS IS HOPE?

Pediatric health care providers have a strong tendency to fight death exhaustively, even at the very end of life. It is as though if we stop, we are giving up not only on the child under treatment, but on future patients as well. To a degree, this makes sense. In the last decades we have seen gratifying improvements in the survival rates in pediatric diseases that were once always fatal. The cure rate of childhood leukemia, for example, has gone from 40 percent to over 80 percent in the last forty years, and that is largely because of the very aggressive treatment of children no one thought could be cured. We in the field look back at those physicians, and the parents and children involved, with intense gratitude. One of the greatest joys for a doctor is working with a seriously ill patient and watching him get better, knowing that you've helped him survive. When that patient is a child, the joy is even greater.

But sometimes it doesn't happen that way. The illness worsens despite treatment, and a turning point is reached when the disease process has become the dying process. At this time, it is important to question the usefulness of the treatments that are being used. Sometimes the treatment causes horrible suffering and offers only a brief, painful extension of life. When treatment is stopped at this stage, the child's death is not the parents' or doctor's failure, but a natural end to a life with serious disease or injury.

When the turning point is not acknowledged, talked about, and planned for, the child receives further treatment to try to cure him—treatment that may result only in emotional and physical suffering. Attention stays on the medical present and not on the future. Families may have no opportunity to think about the things the child may want to do in his remaining time, things that may require stopping curative therapy.

Where is the hope? The main hope, of course, is that your child will survive his illness, put it behind him, and live a normal life—one that will be richer because of the strength, wisdom, and courage he has learned, and the intensity of the bonding he has had with you as you cared for him.

But what of the child who doesn't survive? Hard as it may be to believe, there is hope even here. Listen to the words of some parents who said it well—Mike and Amy, whose 8-year-old boy was dying of a brain tumor: "The hope is that our child will live fully and comfortably until death. The hope is that our child will fulfill his desires before death. The hope is that our child will die peacefully."

❧ Chapter 1 ❧

Facing Your Child's Life-Threatening Condition

We parents depend on others to educate us during the intense time of living with and loving a child who has a life-threatening illness, and especially when the threat of death turns into the reality of death. We need social workers, doctors, and nurses to gently educate and support us through the process.

*P*revious writings on death and dying, and on grief, identify "stages" of emotional responses through which adults pass as they deal with their own end-of-life diagnoses. Elisabeth Kübler-Ross introduced the stages of denial, anger, bargaining, depression, acceptance, and hope that many experience.* Although people do not go through these stages in any predictable manner, the families of children who have

---

*Elisabeth Kübler-Ross, *On Death and Dying.* Macmillan Publishing Co., New York, 1969.

life-threatening conditions experience similar stages in ways that vary with each family's particular situation. As with the stages of any form of grief, these aren't necessarily experienced in any particular order. Furthermore, the parents of a child diagnosed with a life-threatening illness go through these phases more than once, as the child goes from diagnosis, to remission or symptom control, to relapse or complication or exacerbation, to possible second remission, and eventually either to recovery, or to death.

Complicating this even more is the fact that spouses, siblings, grandparents, and other loved ones are going through their own emotional phases, on their own timetable. There is no single way for this process to occur. The information that follows can help each family create its own action plan. (We are defining "family" here as anyone close to the child: This can include the child's closest friends or the family friends who have functioned as "aunts" or "uncles" in the child's life.)

If your child has been diagnosed with a life-threatening condition, you are trying to care for her at the same time that you are dealing with your own emotions. It is helpful to consider this the beginning of a new phase of your family's life. Whatever course your child's illness eventually takes, everyone involved will be going through a time of emotional, spiritual, psychological, and physical struggle.

How can you find a sense of balance and some peace in the midst of the horror of your child's serious condition? You can step back and remember that you as a parent know your child better than anyone. That has not changed. Your parental instincts will not leave you. It may feel like they have: Suddenly doctors and nurses are in control of so much of your child's life. But remember that your parental instincts have served you well in the past and will continue to do so. Your role as your child's guardian and protector has not been taken away; it is only being partially shared by experts in health care. If you need to, keep reminding the health care team of your role as parent, and of your expertise on the needs of this particular child. You are a participant on the care team, and in many cases the medical profession formally acknowledges this by calling it "family-centered care." But acknowledged or not, it is both your right and your obligation to your child. Whether she recovers or dies, you will know you did your best.

What follows is a discussion of some of the emotional states commonly experienced by parents of seriously ill children. Several of these states can exist simultaneously, but one or another will dominate consciousness at various points in the process. These reactions are a natural human response to facing the harsh reality of a child's life-threatening illness. Shock is usually followed by disbelief, grief, and anger, and most parents will move back to these first four reactions even when experiencing aspects of healing and understanding. Often parents spend a lot of time in the states of disbelief and grief, without realizing they are in shock over the diagnosis and the truth that recovery is not going to happen. You do not need to label each emotional reaction that you or your child is having, but the awareness that these reactions exist can help you to understand your response to what is happening to your child and your family, and to you. Recognizing and accepting these emotions as normal will help you in your attempts to be at peace with yourself and your loved ones.

Inevitably when a parent first learns of her child's life-threatening condition, she reacts with shock and disbelief. "This can't be happening to *my* child!" "Clearly, the doctors have made a mistake." Shock is a protective mechanism: It's a healthy, normal response that allows you to take in the meaning of the doctor's words in absorbable portions.

But if it's not recognized for what it is, shock can prevent parents from hearing and digesting medical information. Your doctors may have to repeat information several times. Even then, you might not really absorb it. Many parents, when in shock, go numb and nod their heads during conferences where medical information is being discussed. Sometimes the doctors and nurses interpret this to mean you understand when you really don't. Sita and Ahmed, the parents of a 14-year-old with leukemia, had a conference with the medical team. A month after the diagnosis, they had another conference with the medical team to discuss the progress of his treatment. The doctors told them that Jahal's chance of survival was only about 30 to 40 percent because his disease had not responded to therapy. They said he would need a bone-marrow transplant.

Sita had nodded quietly during this meeting, and she seemed quite stoic. Afterward, she sat alone with the team social worker. As they talked, the social worker realized that Sita had blocked out what the doctors had said.

"How are you feeling?" she asked gently.

"Oh, fine," Sita said. "Just a little numb. But I don't have time to talk to you now—it's time to pick up Jahal's prescription."

Realizing that Sita really hadn't understood the choices that were presented to her, the social worker arranged for another meeting between Sita and the doctors, and this time Sita was able to take in the reality of what was happening. It took many meetings, but ultimately Ahmed and Sita were both able to understand the new treatment. Jahal had the transplant, and it worked. As of this writing, four years later, he is a healthy teenager, playing basketball on his high school team and planning for college.

When you're told that your child probably won't live, the shock can be far worse. The mind protects you from the unthinkable by simply erasing it. Parents may insist that the diagnosis or prognosis is wrong. Again, this is a protective mechanism, but it can be counterproductive if it lasts too long. The 10-year-old patient of a colleague died while his parents were still insisting that the doctors were wrong. Even as young Andrew was painlessly slipping away, his father was calling for the doctors to revive him. As a result, he missed the opportunity to really be with his son at the moment of his death, and to experience how peaceful that death was.

Because shock and its consequent emotional paralysis can produce the false impression that you understand what you are being told, you need to realize that you can and should go to your doctors later with a list of questions. (Step B will help with this.) This is a major part of getting the information that you need to make good decisions. It will take time for the shock to wear off and for routine questions and obligations to make sense. Like all emotions, shock comes in cycles. It becomes more bearable to face reality as this emotion ebbs and flows with time. In addition, keep in mind that at certain times you may simply not be able to deal with routine conversations and decisions. This, too, is completely normal. In time, when the harsh and numbing states of mind pass, you may need extra support in order to accept yourself and your emotions as they are. It's a bit like the way an anesthetic wears off after an operation: As the numbness wanes, the deferred pain asserts itself.

Sometimes, however, the denial that comes with shock remains as its own protective mechanism. You determine to rise above this disease and defeat it once and for all. Midnight computer searches for a cure your doctor doesn't know about, third and fourth opinions, and book after book about miracle cures may consume you. In the beginning, this can be useful. You might indeed learn more about your child's condition, even about other possibilities for treatment and cure. But eventually you'll have learned all that you can, and you'll need to come to terms with the limits of the situation. Focusing on the search for a nonexistent answer can prevent you from dealing with the essential emotional, psychological, and spiritual issues that confront you and your family. Further, the desire to cling to your child's life can induce you to accept treatments with little or no therapeutic value, instead of concentrating on things you can do that actually may help your child. There are some treatments that only increase the suffering, creating terrible side effects. You'll need to learn an extremely important skill at this time: How to distinguish between a genuinely useful treatment and one that cruelly creates the illusion of hope when no real hope exists or even significantly diminishes the quality of your child's life. As one woman, whose son eventually died of cancer, told me, she and her husband spent all their time in pursuit of the miracle cure. "We convinced ourselves that the cure was out there, but the doctor was just too lazy to find it," she told me. They tried many different treatments, none of which worked. In spite of the increasingly obvious fact that the boy was declining, his death came as a shock to them. What gnaws at them now is wishing they had known he was dying, not their choice to keep looking for treatments.

None of this means that it is wrong to proceed with "experimental" therapy. Some of these therapies work, extending or even saving lives. But it's crucial to have clear, reasonable goals for the treatments that you as parents choose with your doctors. Such goals include a rational hope for cure or for more time, or a decrease in pain or suffering, or both. Try to keep in mind whether a particular type of treatment does something "to" your child or "for" her. Ask the doctors to help you prioritize treatments in this way, by asking utter honesty of them and of yourself. If you can do this, you have a valuable tool for making your choices. A promising new treatment may indeed turn the tide and save your child's life. If not, even a few more weeks of life for your child may be worth painful side effects. Sometimes a trial of treatment to see if goals are achieved is reasonable. On the other hand, a better quality of life may be more important than this extra time. Also ask whether the treatment will keep the child in the hospital. For some children and families, extra time alive spent in the hospital is a boon, and for others, nothing is worth having to spend extra days in the hospital and the child will be happier spending her last days at home. Whatever you decide, do it for your child. If she isn't an infant or isn't mentally impaired beyond the ability to reason for herself, try to make her an active participant in any decision. It's her life—and, if no treatment can save her life, it's her death.

No decision is inherently right or wrong. Aggressively treating advancing disease and accepting the hardships of treatment may be the best thing for a particular child and family. People who tenaciously cling to life can often accomplish near miracles, especially when they have a specific event to live for. We have all heard stories of children who have lived far beyond their prognosis. I would never discourage a parent from holding onto hope.

But at some point, it may be wiser to accept that the time for the miracle cure has passed. You may need to adopt additional goals: another day or week of life, or the chance for your child to say good-bye to family and friends, or the opportunity to live long enough to achieve some dream, such as attending the prom or seeing a World Series baseball game. Above all, perhaps, is the goal of keeping your child pain-free and helping her live peacefully through whatever time she has left.

The family of a 6-year-old boy a colleague worked with could not acknowledge the advancement of Tommy's cancer.

Grasping for a cure, they continually added treatment after treatment, each leaving the boy more and more drained, so fatigued that he was eventually unable even to sit up in bed. They could not conceive of his dying from the cancer, nor would they listen to the medical staff who warned them that he could actually die from the effects of the treatments they had convinced themselves would cure him. In fact, he finally died from a treatment-related infection. The family never had a chance to say their good-byes to him. The doctors encouraged their attitude, calling it "going down fighting." The father is still very bitter, months after the boy's death—bitter not at the choices for continued treatment but for missing the chance to talk with his son about what was happening to him, and to say good-bye.

It doesn't have to be that way. The family of one of my patients who had advanced cancer talked with us about the possibility of radiation therapy, which might have produced several more months of fairly good quality time (but with some significant side effects). "Doc," the mother asked me, "would you be mad at us for not doing the radiation?" Of course I wouldn't, I assured them. The family opted instead to bring their little girl home with them, and to make her last few weeks special and happy. In the process, they were creating important memories for themselves—happy memories that have helped soften the edges of the sad ones. She died peacefully at home. The parents still grieve, but are at peace with their decision.

Most parents will feel anger during the various phases of their child's illness. You will probably be angry at the unfairness of your child's suffering, at the very thought of her mortality, at the loss of normal family life, at the rest of the world for going on normally.

If it becomes clear that your child will die from her condition, your anger may grow into fury. And it will not always make sense. You may be angry with the doctors for not curing your child, at your friends for having healthy children, at yourself for letting this happen. You may even be angry with the child herself for getting sick. It's important to let yourself feel all your anger without guilt or judgment, but with evaluation. Has the doctor really neglected something that could have helped your child, or simply failed to perform a miracle? Was there really anything you could have done to prevent what happened to your child? The answers will probably be no, but you need to allow yourself to ask.

People often become angry with their God at this time. Spiritual questioning is a normal process under these challenging circumstances, and anger is a natural part of that. As isolated as you may feel from your particular faith, seeking out a spiritual advisor or religious leader can be extremely helpful. They will not be disappointed in you for questioning things; they are used to hearing doubt and rage, and their assistance can often be invaluable. (This will come up again in Chapter 5.) My chaplain colleagues tell me that the guilt associated with feeling anger at God, even if it is not expressed, can magnify the anger. The simple act of naming this anger, and admitting that it is there, can result in a sense of freedom. It won't take away the anger, but it can help you to be able to make decisions even when experiencing it.

"One of the greatest struggles for many people is reconciling something as horrible as a child with a terminal illness with a kind, loving, and compassionate God," says The Rev. Paula V. Mehmel, senior pastor at St. Martin's Lutheran Church in Casselton, North Dakota. "Even people of faith become angry with God, wondering how or why this happened." Sometimes, she says, they demand to know how God could cause this to happen. "This is both normal and in many ways healthy for people," she adds, "especially if they move through the anger by talking about it. It becomes worse when a person feels guilty because of it. Denial and guilt often drive a wedge between a person and God. But God," she emphasizes, "is big enough to hear our anger, support us as we struggle, and listen to whatever we need to say in our prayers." And God doesn't "take notes on us and come back later and get even for our angry outbursts."

But for anyone of faith, being angry with God can be useful. "It keeps the conversation with God going. I believe it is only in that process of talking with God and being open with God that true spiritual healing can begin to occur for any family who faces the death of a child."

This anger may get in the way of your being the kind of parent you want to be right now. Give yourself a break, and remember how normal this emotion is. Remember that "keeping a lid on things" can become more difficult as time goes on. And you may not be hiding your feelings as well as you think. Before your anger emerges in destructive ways, use professionals, or your friends, to help you to find an outlet for this.

Another frequent response to learning of a child's illness is grief. We think of grief as something that happens after the fact: Someone dies, and after that we grieve. But there is also anticipatory grief. The fact that a child has a life-threatening illness can evoke this. You mourn the loss of security and the possible loss of some of your child's mobility or functioning.

When parents are told that their child will surely die, their grief is shattering. Most people say it is the worst thing that can happen in the human experience. So I tell you now what you most likely cannot believe, but what is mercifully true: You can survive. Your life will be permanently changed, and grief will always be part of it. But you will be okay. You will get through it and there will be help from many directions.

When you have begun to realize all the potential loss your child's illness threatens, you have entered this grieving stage. Different members of your family will come to this stage at different times, depending on the type of disease or injury your child has. There is no right way to grieve. If you are trying to find a cure for your child with an experimental therapy, you may find that some of you are experiencing hope, while others are grieving the child's approaching death. This can be hard, because you need your feelings to be validated, and this is less likely to happen if your spouse or parents are going through different emotions and different expectations. You can get help from the social workers, the psychology team, or pastoral counselors who work with your child's doctors, and from your trusted friends.

Reaching out to such people is crucial. You need to get help from anyone with whom you can share your deepest feelings, or from whom you can derive the most comfort. Grief can be extremely isolating. Unfortunately, not everyone feels comfortable talking about these things. If your friends can't give you what you need, ask your medical team to refer you to people who specialize in the field. This is discussed in Steps C, D, and J.

Your child needs help with this as well, as do her siblings. The children are grieving, too. Even if they haven't been told what's happening, they'll realize that something is terribly wrong. The inevitable family disruption, the pained facial expressions, the unexplained tension—all tell children that something of enormous consequence is happening. There are professional staff (child life specialists, child psychologists, social workers) who can make a real difference for your family in this situation. They can help you to talk to your ill or injured child, her siblings, her cousins, at a level that is right for each child's age. An important and impressive lesson we learn over and over again is that the children usually handle it better than the adults think they will. Talking with them will help them to deal with the current situation, and to face their loss when the child dies. (This is discussed further in Step I.)

The family of one 3-year-old girl, Cheryl, learned that their daughter's brain tumor was not responding to treatment and that she would probably die within two months. Her parents were very open to receiving help with their grief, and counseling sessions for them were quickly expanded to include Cheryl's 14-year-old brother, Jason, and her 6-year-old sister, Meryl. The hard work they did included tearful sessions looking at the family photo album.

They were able to go through the final weeks of her life as a close family and saw the importance of creating special experiences together as they did so. They took many photographs during this period, solidifying the time they had with Cheryl in all their memories.

If it is clear that your child will die of her condition, you and she both face the difficult task of letting go—facing the inevitable and making the time you have together as meaningful as possible.

For the parents, coming to terms with the fact that their child will die involves facing the medical truths. In daily life it is helped along best by the child's natural ability to live one day at a time—something you need to learn from her at this time. If you as a parent can tap into this ability, and if you have been working with the medical team to make sure your child is as comfortable as possible, you can more readily deal with what is happening.

Older children or adolescents will express their many feelings in a number of ways. They may be feeling as much rage, confusion, and fear as you are. As they come closer to acceptance, they may have many quiet days, with a lot of thinking going on. Often they use writing or drawing as a way of expressing these things.

Our team worked with a courageous girl of 17 who was dying from a recurrent brain tumor. There was much on Letoya's mind. She told her parents and counselors that she was angry with friends whom she felt had deserted her during her illness. She also talked about the friends who had held fast, and how she cherished them. She needed to have "one more sleepover" party with the friends she loved best. She was able to express her anger, her love, and her eventual resignation. She had her sleepover: "It was great," she told us happily.

There is another aspect of anticipatory grief and letting go with this age group. The older child may want to retain some measure of control by "owning" her disease. She will want to be in charge of what happens each day and may not always want to talk about it. She might seek the opinions of friends or medical team members before yours. It's hard, at this time when you most want to help your child, to instead let her take over. But be proud: She is doing the only growing up she'll ever have a chance to do. Allow her to master her own disease, letting her know that you're still there whenever she needs you.

It is tremendously important for the parent of a dying child to come to terms with the job she has done. This means accepting the job you did as a parent, without judgment. It involves a review of the kind of parent you have been, and a look at your mistakes. It helps you to recognize that you have done your best, and to learn how to forgive yourself for whatever mistakes you made.

It also involves accepting the job you did *as the parent of a seriously ill child.* You can be proud of yourself. You have been doing the hardest job any parent can ever do. If you have any unresolved issues about the management of your child's illness, talk them over with the doctors now; get your spouse or a close friend to do that with you, if you find it hard to do alone. If your child's symptoms haven't been controlled as much as possible, that has *not* been your fault. The medical world is struggling to teach doctors and nurses how to better control pain. You've done your best through this illness—give yourself credit for that. (This is discussed in Step N.)

For your child, acceptance may now involve looking at her relationships with family and friends throughout her life. This may mean spending special time alone with people other than you. Parents sometimes resent precious time away from their child when there is so little time left, but these encounters can help your child achieve closure and a sense of having made a mark on the world, as well as helping people who have also loved her. These can be profound and precious communications.

The ultimate gift that your child can give you is her sense of peace. Just like dying adults, dying children may feel a need to hold on to life until they get "permission" from their loved ones to die. If that's the case with your child, you may need to assure her that, much as you will miss her, you understand that she's ready to leave and that you can accept that. Say something like "I'll miss you, honey. I love you so much. But it's okay for you to let go. Mom and Dad will be all right." It is a very loving act.

Again like their adult counterparts, children may hold on until they have achieved a particular goal. Sometimes this goal is assuring themselves that parents will be okay. One of my colleagues worked with a 14-year-old who was dying of a rare degenerative disorder. Mark was ready to die himself, but he was not ready to risk his father's early death. His father had high blood pressure, and frequently failed to take his medication. Mark made him promise that he'd take his medication after the boy died; when he got that promise, he died peacefully.

One hard part of this process is its uncertainty. No one can predict precisely when death will come. At best, we can make an educated guess. There will be a period of time remaining for your child that is of uncertain duration. I have watched families use this time for simple picnics in the park, board games played at home, special rites of passage. Sometimes they use it simply to be together and talk. I could only marvel at the strength shown by these adults, adolescents, and children. This time was extra special because of the serenity that had come over the families, which made their close communication possible.

It may not seem possible that such serenity will ever occur, either while your child is living or after she is gone. But it can. It is a serenity based on knowing you have done all you could. This book is meant to help you to achieve it. If your child survives, the serenity can remain with you through all the fears you experience that the disease may recur or the injury may happen again. If she dies, it can remain with you through her dying, and in the years ahead.

Chapter 2

Individuality of Disease, of Child and Family, and of Choice

I am Charlie's mother, and the doctors always re-spected that. I felt in charge and was confident in the fact that those who had my trust advised me. It was a comfortable arrangement. I knew my child best.

W e have reviewed some of the difficult psychological issues that confront families with a child who has a life-threatening illness or injury; now we'll discuss some individual steps in dealing with your child's condition. Again, while we proceed in a series starting with diagnosis, these steps don't always occur in a specific order.

STEP A: *Empower Yourselves as Parents*

There is a quote I have taken to heart, written by the father of a dying child in an essay entitled, "This Is My Child, This

Is Your Patient." He says of the medical team, "Not one of you knows our child from the start to now."* His strong statement is a plea for doctors to consider the boy in the context of his particular family, which has been affected by a particular disease. He asks the team to respect the parents' knowledge of their child, thereby validating their authenticity as decision-making participants.

He is right. You are your child's advocate. It is crucial that you empower yourself to make medical decisions in partnership with the medical team (or clinic/hospital) in order to make certain that the child is treated in a family-centered way.

Wise pediatricians teach their medical students to "listen to the parents, for they know their child!" But not all medical providers think that way. They should. And you—as mother or father—should overcome any tendency to defer to the authority of the doctors when you have questions or disagreements and insist that all important decisions about your child's medical treatment be made jointly with you. You should establish this at the time of diagnosis of the serious illness or injury. I have been teaching parents for years that they will be making decisions with the doctors at various points in the illness, based on what they and the doctors know at each of these time points. My hope for the families I work with is that no matter what the outcome, they will be comfortable

---

*Candlelight Childhood Cancer Foundation Quarterly Newsletter, Fall 1989.

looking back on their decisions, knowing they were made with both excellent medical information and excellent parental wisdom.

If you are reading this at the time of initial diagnosis, try to set that kind of goal, and keep it in mind as you talk to the doctors. If you're reading this in the midst of your child's illness, you can still begin to create, and implement, that goal. Even if your child's condition is worsening and you have been told that he is unlikely to recover, it is not too late to start operating that way.

The first step in making your decisions is to obtain good medical information about the condition, the prognosis, treatment options, and the consequences of those options. This knowledge can help you to be effective when you seek information about your child's medical condition, and can allow you to understand it more and more over time. The process can continue as his condition changes.

A good treatment plan can be made only with complete information, and the plan will change as that information changes. So when a treatment plan is chosen, this is not a one-time-only decision. As the condition changes, the plan may need to change. You must continue to ask questions about your child's condition and prognosis throughout the illness. If the treatment does not bring about the hoped-for result, you will want to consider other options. This may be scary, but it can be even more overwhelming (both now and later) if you do not ask these questions. In the next section we will discuss how to ask doctors specific questions so you can get comprehensive information.

One of my colleagues worked with an 8-year-old girl named Emily, who had a complicated heart defect. Her family had a meeting with the medical team social worker on the intensive care unit. There were three different specialists involved, as the child had been worsening after surgery. It had been difficult for the parents to decide to go ahead with the surgery. As Emily's condition changed, the social worker helped to arrange daily conferences with the doctors so that the family could ask new questions each day. This made it easier to organize the information and helped the parents to feel confident in their decisions. Because her recovery from the surgery was rocky, with lots of ups and downs, the parents had many such conferences, which helped them to remain active participants in their child's care. Ultimately the surgery was successful, Emily recovered, and she is now a strong, healthy child.

The choices that parents make in these difficult circumstances are as varied as the people involved. One family I worked with had a 2-year-old daughter whose disease was treated with a therapy that had a 20 percent survival rate. This family chose a bone marrow transplant for Sarah. They were fully informed of the risks, fully scared, fully hopeful, and as prepared as loving parents could be for the possibility that it might not be successful. Sarah's transplant was indeed 100 percent successful and now, several years later, she's fine. Another child, Richard, was on the bone marrow transplant unit at the same time, also with a 20 percent chance of survival. Sadly, he did not survive. But as vital partners in treatment decisions, his parents too felt they made good choices. And in their grief, they do not regret their decisions.

When facing the recurrence or worsening of disease or injury, most parents choose a plan aimed at curing their child. It makes sense, and fits the role of parent, to continue to treat the disease in this way. Once treatment begins, though, the "doing something" mindset can take over: Parents may not want to consider the possibility of the treatment not working, and of the child dying. But if they don't consider it, they can't prepare for it. So when choosing treatment for your child's life-threatening condition, reevaluate treatment options with the medical team at agreed upon points. Promise yourself you will ask them to tell you if it becomes clear that treatment has done all that it can to prolong life. Find out how they will determine whether or not the treatment is effective.

Some families opt not to treat their child's life-threatening disease because they feel that the further attempt to cure disease is not reasonable. Medical culture currently tilts toward the philosophy that no condition is truly hopeless, that there is always some therapy worth trying. Such a philosophy can make parents who don't choose high-tech therapy feel that they are wrong, or bad parents. But when, for example, an infant has a brain tumor that has spread, is it wrong for parents to opt for simply holding and loving their baby for what time he has left, and rejecting curative treatment? I have seen such babies, and I have seen some parents choose instead to embark on aggressive treatment. All of these parents did what was "right"; they did what was best for their children and their own families. They empowered themselves to make the decisions for their children, and they have peace of mind about their decisions.

You Decide: Parents and Child-Patient with Doctors

You should discuss all the treatment possibilities not only with the doctors, but with your family and friends as well. It is important, however, that *you as parents* be the ones to participate in making the decisions with the doctors. And it is important to involve your child in decision-making to the extent that his age, developmental level, and medical condition allow.

Even very young children are capable of participating in such decisions. Rosaria, an 8-year-old patient of one of my colleagues, had a widespread kidney cancer. Her parents had always told her what was going on with her cancer and its treatment and were just as honest when the disease came back after a remission of one year. Chemotherapy was started but was ineffective. When they were offered experimental chemotherapy, Rosaria's parents told her that it would involve time in the hospital, and that if she didn't want to have this treatment, she didn't have to. Rosaria and her family thought about it for a few days, and she decided that she wanted to try it. Rosaria underwent the chemotherapy, spending most of the time in the hospital and managing a few visits home. The team worked as much with pain and nausea control as with the chemotherapy, so she was as comfortable as possible. Though her disease did not respond to the treatment, everyone felt good about having tried it and about Rosaria's ability to participate in the decision. She died very peacefully at home, with her family and hospice nurse at her side. She knew that her parents had done all they could for her, and they were glad they had honored her wishes.

It can be trickier when a child has different feelings about treatment than his parents do. Depending on his age and awareness level, the child's parents may or may not decide to follow his wishes. But it's always good to make him part of the decision-making process, even if you are not able to strictly abide by his desire in the end.

As you discuss the situation with family members, ask for their advice, but do not surrender decisions to them. You will come to your own way of thinking about treatment decisions, and you can choose whether you need to explain or justify decisions to friends and family. Those who love you and your child may find it difficult to accept that your child cannot get well. They may push you to try treatments that you have decided against. They may ask, "How can you just let him die?" Or they may be upset if you choose a treatment they think will be useless and painful. Though grounded in love, such responses may also involve confusion, anger, guilt, or any number of other emotions.

The parents of Jael, a 14-year-old girl with a brain tumor that, despite chemotherapy, was worsening, were faced with this when they decided against radiation therapy. Both Jael and her parents thought that the nausea and fatigue that typically followed such treatment were not worth the small chance that it would help. Jael's grandparents had trouble accepting this decision, and their questioning became more and more difficult for the child's mother. It took a few con-versations with the help of the medical team social worker to calm this situation. Once that happened, though, the grandparents were able to focus on loving and helping their granddaughter, which lightened the load for her parents considerably.

How do you cope with such situations? You remind your loved ones that you have worked with the medical team to get information about what the benefits and burdens of each treatment would be for your child and family, and that you have made your decision after careful consideration. Again, having the medical team meet with your family may be helpful to you as well as to other family members.

There is a lot for you to do and learn now. If your child is rapidly getting sicker, there may not be a lot of time to do it. Or, he may be stable and just embarking on a course of treatment that might or might not prolong his life. Either way, you can accomplish what you need to. You can estab-lish yourself firmly as the doctors' partners. Only by doing that can you be assured that you will be able to maintain a sense of control, working toward the greatest likelihood for recovery, or, if that becomes impossible, toward a peaceful death for your child.

CHAPTER 3

TAKING CONTROL OF YOUR LIFE

The first time you hear it from the doctors, it is like an explosion. You hear how terribly sick your child is, and then you hear nothing else they say because your ears are ringing from the force of the blow.

❧

STEP B: TALKING TO YOUR CHILD'S DOCTORS—THE EARLY STAGES

Your child has been diagnosed with a life-threatening condition. You know you need to make good medical decisions with the doctors, and you know that you have to get—and learn to understand—good medical information to do that. The challenge early on is to do it in the midst of shock, sadness, confusion, and possibly anger. Complicating matters is the possibility that your loved ones may be in different emotional states than you find yourself in.

So let's equip you with the important early questions to ask the doctors. First, we need to give you the tools to make these discussions efficient and effective for you, given the emotions involved.

Most parents of seriously ill children want all the information that the doctors have. Some don't, however, fearing that it will be overwhelming. So doctors do not always assume that you want all this information. If you do, say so. Say, "Doctor, we want you to tell us everything." While it may be hard to hear difficult medical information, there will be fewer unpleasant surprises if you know that nothing will be kept from you.

Realize that your emotions and shocked state will keep you from remembering what to ask. Write your questions down *as they come to you* (keep the list handy; some questions come to you at 3:00 A.M.!). Add to these the questions that your family members come up with. Any question is a good question; there are no "dumb" ones. As a teacher friend of mine says to her students, "The only stupid question is the one you don't ask." More questions will arise after these discussions; when you have subsequent meetings with the medical team, have your new list of questions prepared and you will have a better chance of getting all your questions asked and receiving all the information you need. The medical team won't mind this; it increases their efficiency, too.

Realize that your emotions and shocked state may also make it difficult to remember some of the answers. Things tend to make sense as they are discussed with the team, but after the doctors have gone, facts may get jumbled up in your head as you think about it later. Don't try to remember everything. Write down what you hear, or consider asking a friend or family member to be present for the conversations and to take notes. You may want to bring along a small tape recorder and record the conversation, so you can go over it later. Ask to have these meetings in a private, quiet place.

Try to decide what works best for you in terms of who is present for detailed conversations with the medical team. Having too large a group can get in the way of a good flow of questions, but having a few key friends or relatives present can be very valuable. Aside from taking notes, they may also ask some good questions that will help you get more information. And they can simply serve as support people for you. Further, by learning about the medical issues, they may be able to function as medically competent babysitters for your child.

What are the most important questions to ask?

- Ask the doctor what your child's diagnosis is, in very specific terms. If you don't understand some of the medical words (as is frequently the case with laypeople), ask for precise clarification. Ask for it to be written down. Ask for written information explaining the disease or condition, or for a review article about it. You may feel like you want to gather this information yourself (this is, after all, the age of the Internet). Do this, but be careful. There is plenty of good and bad information on the Internet, and it can be difficult to tell the difference. Internet material may also be outdated. Review with your medical team any information that you find there. Also, your doctor may be aware of cutting-edge, state-of-the-art diagnostic information that is not yet published or widely circulated. Your team can provide good Web sites.

If this information is given to you, ask that it be written down as well.

- Ask specifically about your child's prognosis—her chances of survival or recovery. What are her chances with treatment or without treatment? Where does their information come from? national clinical trials? the experience of the particular group treating your child?

- Ask how your child will be kept comfortable. What will be done to treat pain or anxiety? Ask the doctors, "If my child is sedated, how will we know if she's in pain? Or if she's scared?" It will help if you establish early on that your child's physical and psychological comfort is a primary concern, and that you need information about how these issues will be handled. Further, be sure the plan is communicated to all the nurses involved in your child's care, as they spend much more time with her than the doctors do.

- Ask who is in charge of your child's care. There should ideally be a single doctor (perhaps a specialist or attending physician) who will be in charge of her care throughout the entire illness (or injury, or life-limiting condition). Ask who else will be on the care team, and what their roles are. For example, there may also be a primary nurse or nurse specialist. Other members might include psychologists, pastoral counselors, and home care nurses. Even when the doctors in charge change on a rotation, you need to know whom to go to.

- Ask about treatment options other than those the doctors present to you. Ask what the chances are that each treatment option will work. How fast is it expected to work, and how soon can you expect any changes? Together, you and the doctors will need to set goals (control of pain, cure of pneumonia, removing a tumor, etc.) for each course of treatment. As you gain insight as to the expected timeline, you can ask the doctors to help you know when you and the team should reevaluate the treatments.

- Ask about the expected side effects of the suggested treatments, and how to distinguish them from worsening of the disease. Whenever you see something that you think might be one of these, ask the doctors these questions: Are you worried about this? Why or why not? Is this expected at this time? Does this change my child's prognosis? Does this mean we need to change any part of our treatment plan?

- Ask whether or not this condition is likely to be seen in any other family members. Some conditions are inherited.

- If you don't understand something, either say, "I don't understand that" or "I will have to ask some more questions after I think for a while." There's nothing wrong with not understanding complicated medical ideas at first, and it's important for you to get all the clarification you need.

- Ask how soon the agreed upon treatment needs to begin. Generally speaking, when a child has a life-threatening illness, treatment needs to start very soon. You may feel overwhelmed at the prospect of having to learn so much before authorizing treatment. It will help to remember a couple of pertinent facts. The first is that you can always discuss

things again with the medical team after you have come to a
better understanding of the situation and options. Another
is that just as in learning a foreign language, your skills improve over time. It will be easier to discuss these medical
concerns as time goes on, and as the shock wears off.

In the early conversations about your child's life-threatening condition, sometimes the doctor is talking about one
thing, while you may still be dwelling on other questions. It
is best to stop the doctor and ask your questions. You may
want to ask something scary like, "Is my child dying right
now?" Often parents have such questions swirling around.
This is another reason that having a friend or relative present can be helpful.

You will experience intense emotions during these conversations. It is okay to cry, to be quiet at times, and to embrace your family. If you are feeling angry, it is best to say
something like, "I feel so angry I don't know what to do." It
is maddening that there is so much out of your control, and
out of the doctors' control. We will discuss in the next section how the hospital/clinic team can help you with the
emotional aspects of your child's illness.

These are the basic questions to ask the doctors; many
others will come up. There should be many opportunities to
talk with your child's medical team, and enough time for
your questions. If this does not seem to be happening and
you are uncomfortable with the level of communication,
you need to insist on improving it, whether with the whole
team or with specific individuals.

STEP C: CONFRONTING, EXPRESSING, AND DIMINISHING YOUR FEARS

There are many fears about illness, and about death and dying. Many people involved in your child's illness are affected by these fears: the child herself, you, your child's other parent, your other children, your extended family, your friends, and the medical team. Further, the nature and timing of your child's condition can affect your fears, and how you cope with them. All of these fears are affecting you, and they may be coloring how you deal with this situation. Your child may be at the beginning of a serious illness that requires months or even years of treatment, and you don't even know if she will survive. Or perhaps you are at another stage of this ordeal—facing your child's imminent death. Either way, fear can prevent you from being able to evaluate the situation adequately and then to make well-informed decisions that you will be at peace with years later. And it can prevent you from living in the moment with your child and family, substituting dread and paralysis for love and peace. But understanding how common such fears are can be a useful tool in controlling them.

Your Own Fears as Parents

It is extremely important to face your fears—as well as the anger, pain, loss of control, frustration, and isolation that come with them. Our society seeks to anesthetize any emotional pain, with the result that talking about pain can make people uncomfortable. You may get the message from others that you should not talk about your painful issues. But you should. If you learn to address and deal with them, you can help your child far more effectively. The fears won't all vanish, but they'll be under your control, rather than holding you under *their* control.

It's awfully hard to do this alone. There are professionals to help you to deal with this; ask for help from the social workers, psychologists, and chaplains on the medical team as soon as you're aware of your fear. This may be hard to do; I've seen many people give an automatic "no" when asked if they wanted such help. But it's wise to give these people a chance, even if you don't even know what your specific questions or issues are. They can help you to figure that out. If you are unable or unwilling to use these particular professionals for this, you might try to find an independent therapist to work with you or, if you're already in therapy, to continue working on the issues there. You can also turn to trusted friends, relatives, other parents in peer support groups, or your spiritual counselor.

One common fear of almost all parents in this situation is that their child will suffer. This is agonizing enough when the child is likely to survive. It is even worse for the parent dealing with her child's imminent death. How often I have listened as an anguished parent asked, "Will my child die in pain?" Many parents can't bring themselves to ask it, or even admit it into their own minds because it inherently acknowledges that their child is dying. Yet the fear is there, underneath, unspoken, and tormenting.

You can confront the fear of uncontrolled pain and suffering, with help. Ask the medical team about it. We will talk about specific questions to ask in Step G, but for now, know that the doctors and nurses will give you some of the information you need, and thus relieve at least some of your fear.

You may fear that you will not be able to handle your intense grief if you lose your child. The terror and panic you felt when your child was first diagnosed or injured was already beyond endurance—How can you bear the harder grief of her death? It is important to talk about this fear, and to learn how, and with what kind of help, you can handle what comes.

You might also be afraid that you won't be an effective parent for your ill child and your other children through this ordeal. We address this in Step E.

Sometimes your fear will be expressed as anger. These emotions are easily confused and mixed; both can sometimes end up at the forefront as your mind attempts to disguise the pain. You may be angry with doctors because the disease was not detected earlier, or because they can't cure your child. You may be angry with yourself because part of you thinks you somehow caused the situation—if you hadn't fed her too many fatty foods, or let her play in the rain, or ignored her when she was whiney, she'd be okay now. Such irrational feelings can be as devastating as more logical ones. But if you recognize them, you can remind yourself that they *are* irrational. Allow yourself all your anger: Work with it, release it, and, when you can, realize that there are ways to deal with these utterly normal emotions.

One purpose of the steps in this book is to provide you with the language to deal with your fear that your child may die. It is helpful to discuss and/or express your fears in some way. Swallowing them can prevent you from getting the help you need and will keep you isolated. And too often the medical team just doesn't ask you the simple question, "What are your fears about the days and months ahead?" You may find that the prognosis is good, and thus relieve your fears. Or the doctors may tell you they simply don't know at this stage—and you can face openly the frightening limbo you're in. In the worst scenario, you can begin to face the inevitable with essential knowledge.

So how do you identify and discuss your fears? Sit down and list them, trying to make the list as complete as possible. Some of what you find yourself writing down may surprise you: feelings that you didn't know you had will pop into your mind. Then try to discuss each fear with an appropriate person. This may be your spouse, your clergy-person, your social worker or other counselor, a friend, another parent, or a physician or nurse. Once you have identified that person, take the next step and commit to discussing these things not just this time, but regularly in the future.

The story of one 3-month-old baby girl shows how bringing out these fears can help you to help your child. Tina had a poor immune system and a very bad pneumonia that was worsening fast. As doctors tried to prepare her parents for the possibility that Tina might die, her mother, Gloria, cried out, "I couldn't survive that!" Gloria needed help with her fear, which was preventing conversations about how to best be available for Tina and her two older sisters.

Over weeks, the medical team gently persisted in talking about Tina's possible death, even while continuing strong treatments they hoped would cure the infection. They helped Gloria understand that she would not be alone in dealing with her situation. Gloria began to express some of her fears. Would Tina be in pain? Would she feel that she was suffocating? The team addressed each question thoroughly—including how to help the other children. This led to the family asking lots of questions—they had found that it was safe to bring up what worried and frightened them. The answers to their questions were tough, but the medical team made them realize that they could help each other and Tina during their ordeal. Sadly, they were unable to save Tina's life; she died peacefully in Gloria's arms, after her sisters had said good-bye to her. Though devastated, Gloria found that dealing with her fears had helped her to do what was best for Tina and her sisters, and to realize that she would, in fact, survive this terrible loss.

Your Ill Child's Fears

Parents usually feel that they are supposed to know what their children are afraid of and be able to calm these fears. But it may not be that easy to figure out your ill child's concerns. Children sometimes disguise their extremes of emotion in order to protect their parents. It might help to find a way for yourself or someone else to reach your child, and to show her that sharing her fears will help, not harm, you.

While fears vary from child to child, there are some that are common to most severely ill children. Young children focus on the here and now, and they do this as much when they face illness as they do at any other time. What's going to happen today, they wonder? Is it going to hurt? The reassurance that caregivers will do their best to prevent and treat pain, including that caused by treatment, goes a long way toward helping sick children trust their doctors and their parents.

Never assume that you know what children are afraid of; you have to ask them. For example, members of a teenage girl's medical team saw her crying in the clinic and assumed it meant she was afraid that her newly diagnosed abdominal tumor would prove malignant. But when one member had the sense to ask the girl what was worrying her, it turned out that she was afraid of a catheter that she'd been told they were going to insert into her bladder. The member told her that the procedure would be done under anesthesia, and she was completely reassured.

Children are afraid when people arrive unannounced to do things to them. They need, whenever possible, to be given advance notice of what is going to happen, be it an I.V. insertion or a trip to the operating room. They also need to be told what effects a given procedure will have on them: for example, if a breathing tube for a ventilator is inserted, the child will be unable to talk. If you establish early in your child's medical course that she will be prepared for procedures as much as possible, her fears will diminish considerably. Some children's hospitals have Child Life Specialists, staff members dedicated to that. They use medical play, photographs, dolls with tubes, and conversation and instruction at the child's developmental level to explain medical issues and procedures. This kind of preparation is tremendously helpful to the child, and so to you as her parents.

Children and adolescents with life-threatening conditions are often afraid of dying and leaving their parents behind. They may worry that their parents will be too sad or lonely without them. You can reassure your child by saying outright, "Mommy and daddy are all right. We are sad and concerned about you, but we are going to be okay." Saying such things directly will help a child, lessening her anxiety.

In working with one 14-year-old girl dying from leukemia, our staff found that she was afraid to tell her parents that she knew she was dying. They were in turn unable to discuss it with her. Debbie told us clearly that she wanted curative treatment not for herself, but because "my parents couldn't bear it if I stopped." The experimental treatment failed to slow the progress of the disease. With little time left, the staff helped Debbie and her parents talk about their fears. Debbie was afraid of physical pain. Her parents were afraid to see her in emotional pain. Once these things were addressed, they could use the days they had left together to talk about their love for each other, and assure one another that they'd be okay, and would be together again. And the doctors were able to assure Debbie that they would do all they could to relieve any pain she suffered. This allowed them to use all the pain medication necessary, with Debbie's parents no longer associating the palliative care team with emotional overload or imminent death.

Other fears are as individual as children themselves. How are you to get your child to express these fears? Again there is a role for professionals here, usually Child Life, social work, art therapy, or child psychology staff. They meet and talk with the child, play with her, have her draw pictures, or do some writing. They can show you how to use these methods to learn, at home, what is going on in your child's mind. It's a good idea for the staff to have some of these meetings without parents present, so that the child doesn't hold back in order to protect them. These professionals at times judge that the doctors and parents need to know what they have heard, and with the child's permission may bring it out in the open for discussion. They can also help teach you as parents how to talk with your child about her emotions and yours.

A nice example of this is how staff worked with a 16-year-old boy who was dying from cystic fibrosis. During private time with the Child Life worker, Tom said he was terrified that his lung disease and the pain it caused meant he would die slowly in pain. The Child Life staff reassured him that the doctors would do their best to prevent his suffering, and they had the doctors explain the pain medications available. This seemed to free him to talk to his parents about it.

Your fears and those of your ill child can cause a confusing mix of emotions when you try to decide how to talk to her about her medical condition. Will the child's condition have a permanent effect on her life—leave her with a disability or a predisposition to a recurrence? How will telling her about it affect her current capacity to heal and cope with her condition?

It's especially hard when the child has a terminal illness. You may be afraid to tell your child such a hard truth, no matter what her age. Most doctors who care for seriously ill children advise parents to tell the truth about the initial diagnosis with the help of Child Life staff or other members of the psychosocial team, using age-appropriate terms. This honesty helps establish trust. You can start by simply asking whether there is anything she wants to know.

Perhaps she will respond, "Am I going to have any more surgery or medicine?" You might answer, "No more surgery, but you'll have medicine for the way your tummy hurts." That may be the only question she asks. On the other hand, she may follow with, "Is my disease back?" You can simply say, "Yes." Again, the questions may stop there.

But finally she may ask you if she is going to die. You can help yourself by having thought about your answer with your spouse, the doctors, and the other professionals helping you, especially when the prognosis is unclear. We find fairly often that the child already knows the answer and is looking for verification and a chance (permission) to talk about it. In advancing illness, children know that their bodies are changing, and open dialogue will enable everyone involved to avoid feeling that issues need to be hidden. So, trust your instincts and continue your gentle, honest conversations with your child. You will probably find that she helps you through this. (We discuss this at length in Step K.)

If your child is on a ventilator and can't speak to you, you can still help calm her fears. As you hold hands at the bedside, continue to reassure her of your presence and of your love, with your gentle voice and your continued touch. Tell her outright all the things you want to let her know. She hears you, and she needs to know how you feel. And even though she can't speak, she might be able to communicate through body language—a squeeze of the hand, a series of blinks. If not, she can still be reassured by your presence.

Your Other Children

Your other children's fears will vary depending on their ages. School-aged children may believe that they caused this illness by having wished bad things for their sibling in the past. They may have said "I hate you" or even "I wish you were dead!" They need reassurance that nothing they did caused this terrible thing to happen to their sibling. Tell them that it isn't their fault, *even if they do not ask.*

Children may have a great deal of resentment over all of the attention that this illness has garnered their sibling. If the sick child's condition worsens, they may later feel guilty about this feeling. You can help them by giving them a task to complete that can help their sibling (drawing a special picture, helping you clean her room), and praising the way they've behaved throughout the ordeal. Let them know that it is normal and okay to be confused, worried, and even a little resentful about what is going on.

Opportunities to visit their sibling are important to such children. Being kept from her may cause them to imagine something worse than reality. If they're scared of all the hospital trappings, or of how their ill sibling will look, you can talk with them and prepare them for what they'll see. Again if the hospital has a Child Life staff, enlist their help with this. You can take pictures of the hospital and of the ill child in her hospital bed to show your other children. And you can make visits as long or as short as your children need. Do not be surprised when the visiting sibling(s) opts to spend a short time at the bedside before wanting to step out and pay attention to something else. They will return when ready, and they may need to repeat this back-and-forth process. Be sure to have a support person available just for them, so that when they need to leave the bedside, there is someone they can talk to.

They may be wondering what will happen to them. The change in their routine, and the feeling of isolation that they may have while you're spending so much of your time at the hospital, can make this worse. They may be afraid that they can catch the illness. Assure them that this won't happen. Even though you may be unable to spend a lot of time with them, you can remember to reassure them of your love, and that you care about what they are going through, too.

It can be very helpful to get your children into a sibling or teen support group, if one is available. This is not just to discuss their fears, though it is an excellent opportunity to do so. Teens who have lost a brother or sister to illness tell us that they suffer feelings of guilt for avoiding their sibling, or for demanding attention when their parents needed to be with the sick child. This can also happen in the case of a child who survives: Her illness and its aftermath have still taken up much of your time and attention, and her siblings will still have reactions to that. Help your other children by making these support systems available to them, so they can resolve their feelings and perhaps feel more comfortable making those hospital visits. (The Further Reading section lists books that are helpful as well.)

STEP D: *Taking Care of Yourself and Thinking Clearly*

Your Own Needs

Parenting a seriously ill or injured child who is facing the possibility of death is a huge responsibility. On top of the task of keeping the medical issues straight, you have a wide range of emotions to face. You also need to keep earning money, and you have to keep the household running.

Where is taking care of yourself on this list?

You've probably been so caught up in your family that you've ignored your own needs. But your needs are important, and they belong on that list.

Ask yourself this: How can you take care of your child if you haven't taken care of yourself? For example, you need enough sleep, and you need regular, nourishing meals. When you've been too busy caring for and worrying about your sick child to keep yourself well rested and well nourished, everything looks worse. Every fever, cough, or setback that the child experiences looks enormous and it becomes very hard to maintain your perspective. You would do well to realize that getting enough sleep, eating regular meals, and getting out of the hospital for even little bits of time are things you do not only for yourself, but equally for your ill child. You'll do more good for her if you're in good shape—it's that simple.

I have never met a parent who accepts this advice with ease. From the time of their child's birth, parents are motivated and socialized to put her needs above their own; most parents accept this quite naturally. It gets magnified when the child becomes ill, and as the treatment progresses, parents put their own needs, goals, and plans aside, assuming that these will be attended to when the ordeal is over. But the ordeal may last months or even years, before your child either recovers or dies from her illness or injury. It's one thing to defer your own needs for a day; it's quite another to ignore them for months at a time.

Of course, it's not easy to find time for yourself when so much time and energy need to be devoted to your child. But there are some things you can do to take care of yourself that don't take a lot of time, and won't take you away from her for long periods.

First of all, you need to get some real sleep. Most children's hospitals have a place for parents to sleep that is close to their child. If you can get undisturbed sleep there, fine. Often, though, this sleep is interrupted. A good night's sleep at home can make a big difference. Can you take turns spending the night at home while another caregiver stays at the hospital? Mothers in particular often find this idea hard. But try it once. When you see how much better you feel, and how much more energy this gives you for your ill child and your other children, you may consider doing it more often.

One family I worked with had a fabulous solution to this. A close family friend held a "sleepover" at the hospital with the child, complete with videos and treats. Her son, a friend of the sick child, stayed as well. Both parents remained home, had quality time together, and slept better than either of them had in weeks. And their son had a special evening with his friends.

Of equal importance, you need to pay attention to your nutrition. The stress of this kind of situation often takes away a person's appetite. Over time, insufficient food intake can harm your body. You must remember to keep drinking fluids (don't make it water all the time, since fruit and vegetable juices provide many necessary nutrients). Sodas are fine for an occasional treat, but emphasize nutritional drinks. Try not to miss a lot of meals. Snack frequently, eating foods with protein and other nutrients. If your friends and family are asking how to help you, ask them to pack and freeze snacks and portable meals for you.

And people often do want to help. No doubt you have been asked, "Is there anything I can do for you?" You probably said "no" before the offer was even completely made. That is the gut reaction of most parents whose child is seriously ill, because your friends and relatives cannot give you what you most want: a cure. But there are many things these people can do for you, and doing these things helps them to deal with their own emotions. They want desperately to be able to help you and your child. Let them. (There may be other friends who turn away from you at this time; we address this issue in Step P.)

Let people do your laundry and clean your house. Let them bring meals to your home and to you at the hospital. Let them sit with your ill child for an hour while you go out for a walk. Let them spend the night with your ill child, or baby-sit with your other children. Let them shovel your walk or mow your grass. Let them make (or take) the phone calls to and from the many people who want to know how you and your family are doing. Let them just be with you. Ask them to keep you in their prayers. These are the more common needs; you will also have needs unique to you and your family. It is best to keep a written list of needed tasks; a friend can keep track of these tasks for you and assign specific things to specific people. Brainstorm with that friend to figure out what you really need from others, and let her be in charge of assigning jobs from the help list.

If you don't have enough friends or family for all the help you need, another source to consider is your church, synagogue, or some other community group.

If you are continuing to work at your job, you have an additional burden. It is very hard to be away from your ill child and the rest of your family. Especially if you are a single parent, you probably feel needed in more places than one. Be sure to find out about the Family Medical Leave Act, and about other resources that are available to you. The social workers can help you with this. Also ask about the availability of respite care. This will vary around the country, but the social worker and your child's medical team should be able to give you some information.

The medical team may have some other supports they can offer as well. For example, there may be discounted motel rooms, or family houses such as the Ronald McDonald House. There may also be discounted parking and meals available. Far too often I have watched parents try to do everything on their own. You are engaged in a difficult and draining experience; ask for help.

Relaxation and Coping

Although it may seem at first to trivialize your situation, and feel like an impossible task, "taking it one day at a time" is important from the moment that your child is diagnosed with a life-threatening condition. At that time, you grapple with uncertainty about her prognosis and start to worry about the upcoming hours, days, weeks, months, and years. You need to slow these thoughts down. You can help yourself by remaining in the present more than you are perhaps accustomed to. Remind yourself that you do not have to decide or deal with anything that is not absolutely necessary today.

Over the course of your child's treatments, there is a very important resource available to you. This is the hospital's psychosocial team. They may have different titles where you are, and their services may not be suggested early on, as the medical team focuses on your child's physical condition. So you may need to ask about them. Don't hesitate to do so. Your needs may vary; consider early meetings with the social workers, Child Life Specialists, chaplains, and psychologists. Later we will discuss what they can do for your family, but now, think about what they can do for you. As you meet them and learn how they will help your whole family, keep a list of their names and phone numbers in a handy place. Your need for this staff will change over time, and they *do* want you to call on them. They are there *for* you and you are *not* a "bother."

The psychosocial team will have several suggestions for helping you to cope. An important one will be the use of relaxation techniques. It can be very helpful to spend time quieting your mind each day. Twenty minutes, or even five minutes twice a day, of silent relaxation, meditation, contemplation, or prayer might quiet your mind, comfort you, and help you to meet and make the decisions that confront you daily. Even a few minutes of deep breathing slows your heart rate and relaxes your muscles. Find quiet, solitary places for this (the hospital chapel, for example).

These professionals can help you to try various other relaxation and imaging techniques. The easiest are those that have you simply sit in silence and pay attention to your slow, quiet breathing. Focusing your mind on a favorite calming image, or on counting, is often used. At first, your thoughts will return to the stressful things going on. You can slowly learn to let these go, and return for a time to peaceful quiet. Don't be discouraged if it takes you a while to learn to do this; it's worth the time and practice for the relief and rejuvenation it can bring.

The Child Life staff will be especially interested in helping your ill child to learn some visualization techniques to help fight the disease or to combat pain (see below). This is something you can learn to do for yourself as well. During your quiet time, visualize yourself in a place that is particularly peaceful for you, or a favorite place where you have been, one associated only with happy memories. (Many people pick mountains or the seashore.) You will want to slow your breathing for this exercise as well.

Kate, whose 9-year-old daughter was undergoing therapy for leukemia, became very skilled in helping Jessie with relaxation techniques during her spinal taps. Kate would take Jessie through the visualization of many different calming scenarios; they were a very creative team. On one occasion, Jessie asked her mother which was her favorite scene to imagine when she herself needed to feel better. Kate admitted that she had not been using relaxation techniques for herself.

"Well, why not, Mom?" Jessie demanded. "If it's good for me, I bet it's good for you too!"

Kate had the sense to do what many of us parents don't do: She took her daughter's sound advice. She began to use the techniques at any stressful time, especially when Jessie had bone marrow tests done to check whether she was still in remission, the test that she found the most stressful. Soon she was able to tell Jessie what her favorite relaxation image was, and mother and daughter were able to share stories of the places they "visited" in their visualizations.

So both you and your child can benefit from finding a good relaxation technique. There are many such techniques, including music therapy, walking/exercise, hypnosis, and yoga. Another powerful technique to consider is affirmation, the use of positive statements to maintain a positive frame of mind. (These are also great when you have little time—you can do a few affirmations while getting dressed, sitting on the bus, or waiting on the checkout line.) This is not to say that you can make yourself happy at a time of grievous stress. You can, however, be positive about your handling of the situation. Tell yourself these truths: "I am doing a good job as a parent," or "I choose peace and tranquility." Ask the medical team working with your child to refer you to the available resources, and remember to ask your *own* physician as well. Sometimes you, your spouse, or your children may experience clinical depression in the midst of all this, and if you do it is wise to seek appropriate counseling and perhaps medication.

🌹

STEP E: HELPING THE CHILDREN TO COPE

The Ill Child

There is a lot you can do to help your child cope with her serious illness. Some of this you can do on your own, once you've learned what ill children tend to think about, want, and fear. Other things you will do better with professional assistance.

It can be very isolating to have something on your mind that feels off-limits to talk about. The ill child whose parents are trying to protect her from emotional trauma by avoiding the subject with her are giving her the message that her illness is a taboo topic. You can help your child by having open conversation about her illness, and about the emotions it brings up in all of you. Allow her to be present during at least some of the discussions of diagnosis and treatment, letting her know that if the discussion is making her anxious, she can leave (or ask you and the doctors to go somewhere else for the discussion) at any time during the conversation. It's fine if you sometimes cry while this discussion is going on; in doing so, you show her that crying is normal and also that after the crying, you are still all right and may even feel better. This approach maximizes trust. If you don't do this, and instead fake a constantly upbeat mood, your child will feel abnormal when she's upset. And she may see a look in your eyes that betrays that good mood and your cheerful words, and feel lied to. If you're honest about your emotions, she'll know she can be honest about hers.

Meera, an 8-year-old cancer patient who was critically ill in intensive care, was being prepared for a procedure when her mother left the room. Meera's family had done everything they could to protect her from the knowledge of her disease and her grim prognosis. Meera told her nurse, "I know why mom left the room. She's going to cry. But don't tell her I know." Meera realized that her parents were sad and worried, but she also figured out that it was not okay to talk about it in front of them. In their attempts to protect her, they forced her to try to protect them, giving her no room to ask them for the support she needed.

By contrast, the parents of Juan, a 7-year-old whose leukemia had come back, and of Alexandro, his 5-year-old brother, were very open with both boys. All through Juan's therapy, they let their sons know how they were feeling. Their whole family was sad together when an infection brought Juan into the hospital, happy together when he achieved remission, and angry and hurt together when the disease did not respond to treatment after a relapse. Juan always felt free to let his parents know what he was feeling at any time, including the emotions involved. Their openness encouraged his.

You can help your child cope with difficult day-to-day issues by insisting that her humanity be respected. She is a person, not a disease needing tubes and tests. She has the right to have all tests and procedures explained and announced ahead of time (if that is your wish), in a way that she can understand. Child Life staff, or the person doing the procedure, can help you with that, using dolls and diagrams. You can also request that painful procedures be done outside of your child's room, so that the room remains a refuge, free from associations with pain and fear.

It's useful to tell the people who are important to your child about her medical situation, so that they can be involved. For example, her schoolteachers and classmates need to know what's going on. They can visit, send cards, and bring news of the school day's events, so that she feels less isolated. It may become possible, even during advanced illness, for her to be present in school for periods of time: She may want this very much. At minimum, try to arrange a visit to your child's class by a representative from the medical or palliative care team, or phone calls to school to keep the staff informed. If your child is a member of a sports team, a scout troop, a church youth group, or another community organization, it may also be helpful to incorporate those peers and activities into her world as much as possible.

The psychosocial team is as important to your child's coping as it is to yours. She should have someone on the team available solely to her. This may be the child psychologist on staff, her private doctor, a Child Life Specialist, a chaplain, a social worker, or a nurse. These professionals are uniquely qualified to communicate with children at many developmental levels. Such communication is critically important now, as she faces weeks or months of medical treatments and, perhaps, dying.

Without such help, it may be difficult for your child to feel free to discuss important feelings with you. Jenny, a 16-year-old with widespread bone cancer, was facing an experimental treatment that offered her only a small chance of a cure. She herself felt certain that the treatment would be useless, and told the child psychologist that she feared dying in pain caused by the drugs.

"Have you told your parents how you feel?" the psychologist asked.

"No," Jenny said. "They're too full of hope about this drug. I don't want to take it—I'm going to die anyway—but they want me to, and I don't want to hurt them."

The psychologist talked to the other members of the staff, who assured her that her pain would be treated aggressively. Then, the team tried to help the family to have these conversations together. There was too much resistance to that, though. Unfortunately, it was too hard for her parents to talk with their child about her dying, but she did have professionals available to her who could do so, and they were an enormous help.

Some hospitals have pediatric art and music therapists who can assist your child to express her feelings throughout the hospitalization. Creative expression not only benefits the child in the here-and-now, but also gives her the knowledge that, should she die, she has left artwork behind for her friends and family. Sometimes children are able to express things through art and music that they cannot verbalize directly. Donna, an adolescent cancer patient, had been forbidden by her parents to talk about her impending death. They wanted her to "stay hopeful," they told her. But she knew she was dying, and needed to express it. She created, with the help of an astute music therapist, a personalized Christmas carol. Without explicitly acknowledging the song as a memorial, she extracted a promise from her parents that her carol would be sung every year at the family's Christmas party. In this way, she created a lasting memorial of her presence in the family. And she was able to say her good-byes to her family who could not allow her to say them directly.

The Child Life and child psychology staff will be especially interested in working one-on-one with your child. This will be extremely helpful to her, and to you, as it shifts some of the burden off you. When your child and the psychologist are spending time together doing what looks like quiet play (arts and crafts, drawing, painting), the psychologist is actually at work trying to draw out her concerns and fears. The psychology staff can bring to the parents and medical team some suggestions for helping the child, without betraying her sense of confidentiality.

Your Other Children

Your ill child's brothers and sisters will also need help coping with this situation. You can spend time with them when you are letting your relatives and friends relieve you at your child's bedside. Arrange for help with siblings' special needs at home. If at all possible, try to keep their lives and extracurricular activities as near to normal as possible, with help from family and friends. Ask someone to take them on outings that involve quiet time for talking, as well as for simple fun. When well-meaning friends and family members shower your ill child with gifts, tactfully remind them to remember your other children too.

The psychosocial team is also available for them. They may not need one-on-one counseling with these professionals, but you should consider consulting with the team yourself to gather suggestions and resources for the issues and fears they will have. Revisit this periodically; the issues will change over time.

✿

STEP F: CREATING POSITIVE DAYS (SEIZING THE MOMENT)

Depending on how ill your child is, you can have some good times together if you take the steps to make that happen. Perhaps you have chosen to embark on a high-tech or an aggressive form of curative treatment. Your goal may be to cure the disease, to accomplish a specific personal or family goal, or to prolong your child's life in the hope that a cure is discovered in time. The inherent uncertainty in that course of action can lead you in many directions. You are trying to hope for the best while preparing for the worst. Establishing a priority now of making every day as happy and as positive as possible is a way to do this.

Marta, 14, and her mother came to the clinic every day for chemotherapy for her brain tumor. Each time the staff would ask, "Where are you going today?" and wait for an answer they knew they'd enjoy. The two had set up a schedule of daily fun—museum trips, shopping outings, amusement park visits that Marta's physical limitations would allow. "I just do whatever she wants to do each day!" her mother explained simply.

While your child is undergoing treatments, such an attitude may lead you to totally indulge her. However, you do not have to forego all normal discipline. Instead, prioritize the important things in your family's days. Later on, this is one of the things that people are able to look back on as a benefit: They tell their medical staff that they have learned what is truly important in life.

Sometimes it is helpful to discuss things with other parents who have faced similar challenges before. Who else would know exactly how to help you now? You will probably have been told by now that it's a good idea to join the parent support group available to you. You may be feeling inclined to put this off until later, but I would encourage you to rethink that. Some parents find the idea of groups intimidating or distasteful. If this is the case for you, ask if you can be matched to a family with a similar experience. Talking with others who are experiencing or have experienced similar trauma can provide you with meaningful tools to cope.

If you face the possible death of your child, the goal of making the remaining time positive is critical not only to you and her, but to your other children as well. Like you, they will live with this for the rest of their lives. They need to remember some good family times, and joy, amidst the sadness. How gracefully the family handles the unbearable challenge will in many ways live on. The surviving children need to remember days where being a sister or brother really mattered. In the interest of their psychological well-being as they grow up, it may help to give extra thought to this step.

The parents of Kayla, a premature baby, were dealing with going home from the hospital without her while she remained in intensive care, on a ventilator and in very critical condition. Their uncertainty about the future was hard to explain to their two school-aged children at home, and things were very stressful. To cope as a family, they began taking their children on outings "in Kayla's honor" as they waited out the long days to see what would happen. They also brought them to see their sister, and they made good use of pictures to create and keep memories. The happy times held in honor of the baby turned out to be a way to teach the children about coping, and it served the family well. Even after Kayla's death, the family continued to honor her memory in this way.

Creating positive days may mean taking a trip that you would otherwise have put off. Many families that I have worked with have taken one or more family vacations during their child's illness that now provide many precious memories and cherished photographs. On a smaller scale, you can throw a picnic in the hospital room or bring a school field trip right to your child's bedside. For the child who survives, such pleasures help to counteract the gloom and fear that memories of this time can bring. "It wasn't so bad," says one young man, recalling the days when he was in the hospital, extremely ill. "We had a lot of fun sometimes!"

Try to find moments in each day when, despite the enormous difficulties of caring for a child and family facing a life-threatening illness, everyone can feel loved and essential in your family. To an amazing extent, you will find yourself taking your child's cues in this regard, rather than the other way around. Just as you took the time to ask what she was afraid of, here is your opportunity to ask, "What would you like to do today?" Doesn't that feel like a normal question to ask a child? She may just want quiet time with you, which may be the most meaningful time of all.

CHAPTER 4

COMING TO TERMS

We talked to the doctors and nurses lots of times over that week. Things were changing so fast. My husband and I had a hard time deciding about the ventilator, and we changed our minds a few times. But we made decisions then that we can live with now.

*T*his chapter may be hard to read. It can be agonizing to think about the possibility that your child may not survive. I urge you to read through it, because preparing for the worst is always helpful, even when there's no certainty that it will occur.

STEP G: *TALKING TO YOUR CHILD'S DOCTORS: WHEN THE CONDITION HAS STEADILY WORSENED*

Often children recover fully from life-threatening diseases or injuries. But, sadly, sometimes they don't. If you're one of the lucky ones, you won't need to read the rest of this book. Your child will recover, and go on to live a full, normal life.

But that doesn't always happen. There may come a moment, in the course of your child's disease, when you realize that he is probably not going to be cured. This can be very difficult for doctors to recognize, as an ill child can go through medical ups and downs that challenge a physician's ability to predict what will happen. Further, doctors can be blinded by the feeling that if a patient does not get well, it means that they themselves have failed. So the medical team may continue to offer therapy options that have very little chance of changing the course of the disease.

If the turning point, in which the advancing illness becomes the dying process, is difficult for the doctors to recognize, it can be even harder for parents of an ill child to acknowledge it or see it coming. So, for some families, this point comes too late for parents to talk to each other, to prepare themselves, their child, or their families. And sometimes, too late to say good-bye.

In Step B, we discussed the importance of telling the doctors that you want complete information, as well as the usefulness of writing your questions down in advance and recording their answers. We also looked at the role of support people in these conversations. We emphasized the need to obtain specific, written information about the diagnosis and prognosis, and to insist that your child's comfort be a priority.

These principles will continue to be important each time you meet with the doctors. You should ask what the doctors' goals for your child's medical care are now that his situation has changed. You should think *with* the medical staff about your own goals as your child gets sicker. These parental and medical goals change as treatments are tried, and the group makes an assessment of how much each treatment did or did not meet them.

There are several goals that may be identified by the medical team and the family. These include cure of disease, prolonging life (gaining some time, even if recovery is impossible), relief of pain and suffering, improving quality of life, providing a peaceful death, and/or getting support for families and loved ones. Other goals will become clear to you and the medical staff, based on your child's particular situation.

The main issue as your child's disease is worsening is to learn how to get from the doctors an accurate idea of your child's chance for recovery. This means asking how likely it is for the disease process to be changed with treatment and how often children in this stage of this condition recover. The purpose of gaining this information is not to take your hope away, but to give you a reasonable idea of what you can hope *for*. Of course, no prognosis is carved in stone. Doctors have seen amazing recoveries. But they also know how likely, or how unlikely, such recoveries are. Talk to your family, gather your support system around you, and ask the doctors to tell you whether your child is likely to survive. If they say the chance of death is greater than the chance of recovery, ask how soon they think he may die.

In many cases, I have seen that parents do not fully understand their child's prognosis. Parents I have interviewed for this book have also experienced this. The reasons vary. Sometimes they are not told; other times they are told only briefly, at the beginning of the treatment course, when it is too difficult to fully take it in. Their lack of response can be mistaken for a sign that they understand the situation, and the medical staff may not see the need to pursue a painful discussion with them.

I recall vividly what happened with Steve, a 12-year-old who had been born with a severe immune deficiency that caused constant, severe infections. He was also seriously developmentally delayed, and had physical handicaps as well. Permanently bedridden, he could not move on his own, he needed diapers, and his parents fed him through a tube in his stomach. His parents never pitied themselves because of their son's condition: They loved and cherished him deeply. His sister had died two years earlier of the same disease. Steve began to have frequent hospitalizations for pneumonia. At one point, the pneumonia became so severe that he almost had to be put on a ventilator. The doctors tried to talk to his parents about the fact that his disease had become life-threatening. They said that Steve might die during either this crisis or the next one, and tried to help his parents with the decision that had to be made: whether or not Steve should be kept on life-support machines. But the family was angry: They accused the doctors of giving up on their son, and refused to discuss it further. They had lived for years with people hinting that their son would be "better off" dead, and resented anything that suggested his life was less valuable than that of a fully healthy child. Because it was so emotional, none of the doctors or nurses brought it up again.

After a long hospitalization, Steve was discharged with no discussion of his possible death, and no preparation for the next crisis. When his next hospitalization came, Steve's heart stopped suddenly. At a very chaotic "code blue," doctors and nurses rushed in with chest compressions and tubes. But there was nothing they could do for him, and he died. Because his parents had not been prepared for the likelihood that this would be his last hospitalization, they were not with him at his death. There had been no review of memories, and no good-byes.

One of the people I learned a lot from was Carrie, a 17-year-old girl with cystic fibrosis. Because children with this disease have trouble clearing secretions from their lungs, they repeatedly get very severe pneumonia. Carrie's lungs had been damaged by many infections, and she came into the hospital with a particularly bad pneumonia. Her parents met at her bedside with the doctors and nurses who had known the family for all the years of Carrie's illness. They had a painful but honest discussion about the fact that Carrie's lungs were in such bad shape that if she were to be put on a ventilator, she would never again be able to breathe without it. The doctors and nurses felt that she was going to die. They explained the options to the family. It wasn't easy for anyone. All of them, including the medical staff, cried during the discussion. Carrie herself wanted to try the ventilator, and the family respected her choice. A week later, when the pneumonia did not get better, Carrie and her family realized that her condition would not improve, and agreed together that it was time to turn the ventilator off and allow her to die naturally. They worked with the doctors to make sure she was comfortable. Her parents were with her, holding her hands as she peacefully died.

Since these conversations can be very emotional, families often hear things differently from the way the medical staff means them. Questions such as "Do you want us to do everything possible?" are especially difficult, because the word "everything" means different things to different people. You need to zero in on more specific questions. When should the emphasis be on curing or prolonging life, and when should it be on comfort and natural, peaceful death? Whatever the prognosis, it is important not to miss any opportunity to keep your child comfortable. *It is crucial to talk specifically about each treatment,* as we will do throughout this chapter (the ventilators, the medicines, and each kind of catheter or tube), and what it is expected to do for your child.

Follow up each question with a more specific one. If the doctors say, "We think it's time to stop treatment," what precisely does that mean? They may mean it's time to stop high-tech treatment against an incurable condition, but you may think it means they will stop treating pain and discomfort aggressively. If you all focus on your goals for your child, then this kind of miscommunication is less likely to happen. If your doctors' statements leave you with any doubt or discomfort, don't hesitate to ask as many questions as you need.

If the doctors say that your child will probably die, you should secure from them a promise to keep his comfort their top priority, as it is yours. After that, the decisions as to whether to continue life-prolonging treatment or not, in the face of your child's prognosis, can be made with this in mind.

Unfortunately, even after good efforts, pain relief is not always immediately achieved. Some types of pain call for more than one kind of medicine or procedure. This can become complicated, requiring a specialist in pain treatment to get involved, and even then some pain may remain. Opioids such as morphine usually provide the best relief. Parents may think that the use of such strong medicine will hasten their child's death, but when pain is relieved, the quality of a patient's life improves dramatically, which can actually create the will to live longer. When talking with your child's doctors, ask for pain and other symptoms to be controlled as much as possible, regardless of the disease- or injury-related treatment that you decide on together. Some parents and even doctors fear that the child will become addicted to strong pain medicine, so they don't use it soon enough or at effective doses. Such addiction does not happen when these medicines are used to treat pain. Your child may need larger doses of pain medicine the longer that it is needed, and his body gets used to the medicine. This is different from addiction. (This is discussed at length in Step N.)

I will never forget Eric, a 5-year-old I worked with who was dying from cancer that had spread throughout his abdomen, causing him severe pain and keeping him bedridden. He didn't eat or drink much—it made him too uncomfortable. We thought that he would die within a week. Then, we got him started on intravenous morphine, and he improved tremendously. The next thing we knew, he was up playing (with his I.V. medicine in a fanny pack) and eating and drinking again. It was 2 months before he died, time he spent with his parents and sister. We couldn't keep him alive, but we could give him a little extra time, and the comfort to enjoy it.

One of my patients was a 7-year-old with leukemia who became critically ill after she developed pneumonia. Anne was on a ventilator, and for days we didn't know whether she would survive. We told the family that she might die, and helped them to bring her brothers and sisters to be with Anne at her bedside. This preparation involved staff from social work, the chaplain, and Child Life workers. Anne defied the odds and survived this pneumonia—and as of this writing remains in remission. But her family told us later how grateful they were that they had gone through the preparation. The whole family had grown closer during the process.

Because she was treated with this palliative (comfort-based) approach, Anne's illness was far less traumatic for both herself and her family. Unfortunately, at this point in the practice of medicine, palliative care is often confused with terminal care and is reserved only for dying patients. Since we don't always know whether a child will live or die, the exclusive association of palliative care with terminal care may result in such treatment being withheld from a suffering child. But parents can advocate for all the aspects of good palliative care for their seriously ill children. *Why should any child, whatever his prognosis, be denied pain relief?*

Adults facing a life-threatening illness often consider writing a "living will." This involves deciding which medical treatments patients want and don't want to have if the disease worsens. Adults are encouraged to consider these decisions before they become seriously ill, and living wills, or "advance directives," are now being discussed during routine doctor's office visits. Most hospital policies require that they be discussed when any adult is admitted to the hospital, no matter how routine the medical problem.

For children with life-threatening illnesses, these discussions rarely take place in the same time frame that they do with adults. If the child recovers, they may not happen at all. If not, they tend to happen when the illness is declared incurable. Discussions will revolve around whether to start using a particular treatment, or about whether to stop using one the child is already on. Children over eight may be interested in and capable of participating (at their level) in the decision-making process. We should listen to them. I will review here some examples of treatment choices, and the questions that would be particularly helpful for a parent to consider in each scenario. If a particular scenario is not relevant to your child it may still be helpful for you to read it, since it may bring up questions that help clarify your own situation.

The choices that parents face are extremely difficult. It helps to understand that if the condition is steadily worsening, in spite of all medical efforts, your child's body is shutting down in a process that cannot be stopped. You are neither *causing* your child's death nor *choosing* for your child to die as you make choices among medical treatments.

All of the treatments that we will be discussing are medical interventions that should be used only if they are likely

to help your child. They can be helpful if they will potentially cure the problem, delay dying, or provide comfort. But
they should not be used if they have no benefits, or if the
pain and discomfort they create are worse than the potential
benefit. To decide whether they should be used, you should
define goals for every treatment. These might include attempt at cure, prolonging life, short-term support while
there is a fixable problem, and promoting comfort or improving quality of life. You should also ask about the side effects of each medication to help you decide whether a particular goal is worth the discomfort or pain involved.

Breathing Tubes and Ventilators

If breathing has become more difficult for your child, the
doctors may suggest the use of a ventilator (breathing machine). In this treatment, a tube is placed in the trachea
(windpipe) and connected to the ventilator (also called a
respirator), which then breathes for your child. He cannot
talk while on this machine, and will need some sedation
(medicine against anxiety) and pain medication in order to
be comfortable. Usually, the ventilator is used only briefly,
until breathing improves or until he dies, but sometimes an
ill or injured child is on a ventilator for weeks or even
months (for a neurologic condition, maybe years).

Key issues are whether it is likely that your child's breathing will improve and whether he will be able to get off the

ventilator. Often this can't be known in advance, so the machine is used for a trial period. To decide whether or not to use the ventilator, you need to know now how your child will feel on it, and how he will feel without it. It's much easier if you know what to expect and can prepare yourself, your child, and your other children.

The question of a ventilator came up with Sandra, a 9-year-old with a kidney tumor. Attempts at surgery and chemotherapy had not cured the disease. She was being cared for by her family at home, with the help of hospice workers adjusting her pain medication. She was very active and continued going to school. In a conversation about ventilators that the family had with the doctor, they looked at options in various near-future possibilities. They decided that if she got pneumonia, they would use one, since it could help her recover from that illness and give her more time to live. That particular scenario never happened. Later, Sandra developed tumors in her lung. After meeting with the doctors, her parents decided against using a ventilator if her lung tumors worsened, because it could not stop her dying from them, but merely prolong her life for a few uncomfortable days. They were wise enough to be flexible, changing decisions about procedures as her medical condition changed.

If a child is already on a ventilator, deciding whether or not to remove him from it can be difficult. The key question is whether or not it is helping him. If not, the possibility of taking him off it should be seriously considered. For this decision you need to know what his death will be like if he remains on the machine and what it will be like if he does not. Ask the doctors for very clear explanations of both scenarios. Sometimes parents fear that the child on a ventilator will feel that he is suffocating if it is turned off. In the case of a dying child the answer is no. In the dying process there is a natural way that the body slows down and stops functioning. If the decision is made to remove the ventilator during that process, the doctors and nurses will make sure your child is comfortable. Whether he is on a ventilator or not, you will be able to hold your child as he is dying. The ventilator can make this awkward, but not at all impossible.

To review: Ask what things will be like with the ventilator and what they will be like without it. The choice may come up at various points, and this is what you need to know to make an informed decision.

CARDIOPULMONARY RESUSCITATION (CPR)

If your critically ill or injured child is in the hospital and is worsening, it is possible that as the disease progresses, his heart and breathing will stop. This is called an *arrest*. It causes monitor alarms to go off, and unless plans are made otherwise, the hospital staff responds rapidly, with professionals equipped to try to revive him. Someone performs CPR (pushing on the chest at the breastbone to compress the heart and circulate blood). If your child is not already on a ventilator, someone will push air into his lungs with an oxygen-filled plastic bag and a plastic mask that is hooked to the bag and fits snugly over the nose and mouth. They will then put in a breathing tube and start a ventilator. Others on the medical team will start large intravenous lines and give your child lots of I.V. fluids and I.V. medicines to try to restart his heart. If this is successful, he will most likely remain on the ventilator for a time, and you and the doctors will need to discuss what steps to take next.

If the team is unable to get your child's heart restarted and get him onto life-support machines, then he will die during the CPR. This can be frightening to you, because parents are usually outside of the room. (This is not always the case, however, and you should ask where you need to be. If it's possible to be in the room, you might want to be.) Nurses or other providers will be sent to let you know how the efforts at reviving your child are going. Your child may have a cardiac arrest if he has continued to get sicker in spite of receiving excellent treatment for his disease or injury. If your child dies despite CPR, you will be able to hold him and spend time with him after he has died. You can meet with the doctors immediately after it happens, and/or later, to have your questions answered.

CPR is a good idea if there is a short-term, fixable problem and your child will return to the same level of functioning as before. If your doctors foresee no hope of recovery, they may suggest that you consider not having it done if there is a future arrest. This is especially likely if they see the possibility of his getting so sick that his heart stops, and feel that he would die more peacefully without the chest compressions and machinery. They may also suggest this if they need to inform you that the outcome following the cardiac arrest and CPR will probably be very bad for your child's quality of life. Again, what you need to ask the doctors is what it would be like for your child, with and without the CPR, to the best of their ability to predict. You'll want to make your decisions with your doctors in terms of what is most likely to benefit your child.

The decisions regarding cardiac resuscitation and attaching your child to a respirator are among the most difficult ones you will make, especially when the prognosis is uncertain. When the doctors can be definite, it is easier. With an unclear choice, there is no one right answer. In that case, you need to realize that you cannot get it wrong. You can only do what feels right for your child. If you continue aggressive treatment, and he dies during CPR, do not feel guilty or blame yourself. You did your best for him. Now is a good time to remind yourself of that. By the same token, if you decide against CPR and he dies, don't second-guess yourself with a vision of a life indefinitely extended.

Jim and Therese were dealing with the constantly recurring severe pneumonia of their 6-year-old daughter, Faith: This was her eighth hospitalization. The pneumonia was caused by an underlying neurological condition, which resulted in both developmental delay and muscle weakness. The weakness interfered with her ability to cough effectively enough to clear her lungs, causing in turn these frequent, progressively worsening attacks of pneumonia. In her previous hospitalization, Faith had spent weeks on the ventilator.

Her lungs had become severely weakened, and she had very few alert and awake times any more. Now, her doctors and parents met several times to discuss whether CPR would be in her best interest if her heart stopped. The doctors did not believe that either CPR or a ventilator would return her ability to awaken. Somberly, Therese and Jim decided to forego the measures and let their daughter die peacefully and naturally. When the pneumonia worsened, she died at home, in her parents' arms, with a hospice nurse there to help.

Ricardo and Maria made a different decision. Their 7-year-old son, Juan, had cancer in his brain and abdomen. He was receiving experimental chemotherapy and was now in intensive care because of the tumors in his brain. Ricardo and Maria met with Juan's doctors and discussed the question of CPR in the event that his heart stopped. They knew his chances would not be good, but they decided that CPR might give the new chemotherapy treatment time to work, and was worth doing. A few days later, pressure on his brain caused Juan's heart to stop, and the medical team did CPR. His heart restarted, and he was placed on a ventilator. Medications kept him comfortable, but unfortunately his tumors did not respond to the chemotherapy. There was another meeting, and this time Maria and Ricardo decided, with the doctors, to turn off the machines. Juan died peacefully in the hospital, and his parents were glad that they had given him that one more chance, even though it hadn't worked as they'd hoped it would.

The decision about CPR will be influenced by whether your child is terminally ill or critically injured and you have chosen to have him die at home (we will discuss this kind of choice in Step R). Then you should have a referral to a home hospice service that has pediatric experience. The issue of CPR most certainly needs to be addressed, and it can only be discussed with your child's doctors in the context of the resources you will have to help you. Most of the time, it doesn't make sense to call 911 and have CPR done in this situation, but these calls sometimes happen because parents have not been adequately prepared to deal with their child's death at home. To avoid this situation, ask the doctors and the hospice team what to expect, and what needs to be done to provide your child with a peaceful death at home. This will involve filling out a form that states your wishes; this form is used if 911 has been called so that those who respond are aware of the situation. Depending on state law, your child will be registered as an expected death at home, and then police and coroners do not become involved. Ask your medical team to explain the legal issues, which may be different in each state.

Transfer to an Intensive Care Unit

If your child's medical condition worsens and he is having trouble breathing or maintaining his blood pressure, your doctors may consult the physicians that work in the intensive care unit (ICU). Many hospitals have specific Pediatric Intensive Care Units (PICU). Sometimes your doctors and the ICU doctors can predict how much your child's condition will worsen and therefore give you and him time to make decisions about possible transfer to the PICU. But when a child's condition worsens very quickly he may need to be transferred to the PICU with little or no warning.

Because of the need for much specialized equipment in the PICU, most hospitals have separate units or wards where intensive care doctors take care of critically ill children. Although different hospitals operate PICUs in different ways, there are some things they all have in common.

- Children with different types of illnesses will often be cared for in the same unit.
- Some PICUs have individual rooms for each patient, whereas others group two or more patients in a common room.
- Nurses often care for only one or two children at any given time. If the child is extremely ill, more than one nurse and doctor may care for him.
- A room in a PICU often looks different from that in a regular hospital ward. There will be different machines, such as breathing machines (ventilators), kidney replacement machines (dialysis), and many new monitors with alarms. Some of the equipment will be familiar to you and your child; some you may not recognize.
- Your child may require a large I.V. called a central venous line (CVL) if he doesn't already have one. This large I.V. allows the health care team to safely and quickly give your child medications.
- Because PICU patients are very sick, these units often have very specialized equipment, require specialized nursing care, and are very fast-paced, stressful places.

ARTIFICIAL NUTRITION AND HYDRATION
(TUBE FEEDINGS AND INTRAVENOUS FLUIDS)

If your child is clearly dying, as his body begins to shut down, he may reach a point where he can no longer eat or drink in significant amounts. He may take a few bites or sips now and then, but this will not be enough to sustain organ function. Then you might have to decide whether it is in his best interest to give him fluids artificially.

Medical fluids are given in several different ways, and the method discussed for your child will depend on how sick he is, and how long it might be used. Your child might have a permanent intravenous line already (placed by a surgeon, and usually in the chest), and if so that can be used for fluids. Otherwise an I.V. line can be put in the child's arm or leg. This kind of I.V. might last just a few days, or it might be put in so that it can last 5 or 6 weeks.

There are other kinds of tubes, called feeding tubes, used to put fluids into your child's stomach. One sort of feeding tube, called a nasogastric (NG) tube, is placed through the child's nose, and goes down into the stomach. The tube can also go from the nose into the intestine; then it is called a naso-jejunal (NJ) tube. These tubes are soft and pliable; the tube is taped to the nose so it doesn't slip out. If your child is at home and the tube comes out, an NG tube can usually be replaced by a nurse; to replace an NJ might require a trip to the clinic or X-ray department. There is also a surgically placed type of feeding tube that is put directly through the abdominal wall into the stomach, called a PEG tube (percutaneous gastrostomy). This kind of tube, because of the surgery needed to put it in and the infections that sometimes occur, is intended only for expected use over a long period.

As a temporary aid to someone with a fair chance of recovery, these things can be extremely helpful. But they may not be a good idea for someone who is dying.

Once artificial nutrition or hydration is begun, the idea of stopping these fluids can be hard for parents, for the fluids are sometimes talked about as "food and water." Thus it is important to realize the artificial nature of putting fluids into a person through tubes. The body's natural response is to stop taking in things it cannot handle and the brain stops sending the cues—hunger and thirst—that it's time to eat or drink. So your child will not be starving or dying of thirst. In fact, during the dying process, the kidneys slow down and make less urine, with the result that any fluid the kidneys don't process can build up in the lungs and other tissues; artificial fluids will just add to the problem. This can bring about difficulty in breathing and cause body swelling. Ask the doctors and hospice team, if you are using hospice, to describe how this applies to your child, and to help you decide when to slow down artificially delivered fluids.

Keep reminding yourself that this is *not* the same as "not feeding" your child. Even if you don't put fluids in I.V. lines or stomach tubes, you still will have food and fluids available at your child's bedside should he want a drink or a little something to eat for pleasure or emotional comfort. Talk about it with the medical team so that you can make the decisions with good information.

Michael, a 10-year-old dying from a brain tumor that had come back very fast, was receiving fluids in his I.V. line as his parents and grandparents held him. He was breathing easily and was not in pain. Most of the time he was asleep. In a few days his body began producing less urine, and his breathing became raspy as the fluid from the I.V. built up in his lungs. As this started to happen, the family met with doctors and together they decided to stop the I.V. fluids, since they were doing more harm than good. He took a few sips of water, but didn't want anything else when he was awake other than to be held. He died peacefully and comfortably, with his parents beside him.

OTHER TREATMENTS

There are other treatments that you may be asked to think about at this time. For each of these, ask the doctors what its benefits might be, and how your child will feel with and without each one of them. As always, ask what the goals are, and what it will be like for your child if you choose this treatment, or if you reject it.

One of these is the use of extra oxygen, which is given through a tube to the nose, or through a mask over the nose and mouth. If your child's illness causes his lungs to stop giving his blood enough oxygen, he may feel better with extra oxygen. However, some children are bothered by the tube and prefer to have it off. Your doctors can help you decide if it's worthwhile. It can be available to use when desired, because the oxygen tanks and the tubes are easy to move around, so your child may be able to use it off and on as he wishes.

Another treatment that might be suggested is antibiotics (usually given by I.V.). For example, a child with heart disease, cystic fibrosis, cancer, or a neurologic disorder might be too weak to breathe strongly, so pneumonia could develop. Antibiotics might help, although in some cases they're useless. Ask the doctors whether they think the antibiotics would truly make any difference to your child's survival or his comfort.

Sometimes blood transfusions are an option. During the treatment for several conditions, especially cancer, transfusions of red blood cells or platelets are routine. This can make the difference between living or dying, or can extend life significantly. But when a child is dying, transfusions will not keep him alive. It's possible, however, that blood transfusions will make your child more comfortable, or less fatigued, and that platelet transfusions will reduce the possibility of bothersome bleeding, like nosebleeds.

The use of certain tubes might need discussion as well. For example, some medical problems cause painful pressure in the stomach or intestines. Having a tube inserted from the nose down to the stomach may relieve that pressure. Also, if your child is too weak to use the toilet, he may benefit from a tube to remove urine (a Foley catheter), though diapers are another, less invasive option.

If your child's health is declining, decisions about these treatments will probably change over time. Try to work with your child's doctors to decide what the goal for each treatment option, at each phase of your child's illness, will be. Once the chances for a cure or for significantly prolonging life are minimal, always remember that the goal is to make things more peaceful for your child.

❧

STEP H: PALLIATIVE CARE AND HOSPICE

Palliative care has traditionally been defined as care that addresses the physical, emotional, psychological, and spiritual needs of people who are dying. Health care systems are now expanding the definition to include this comprehensive service for anyone with serious illness, not just those who are dying. Since this larger definition is fairly new, there is still some confusion about it. A "palliative care service" is sometimes made up mostly of providers who help only with control of pain and other symptoms for the dying. But you need to know that there is palliative care available for your child, *whatever* his prognosis.

Hospice care remains defined as care by a team focused on a patient who will die, and that patient's family. Some programs are defined as "hospice and palliative care." In such a case, a palliative care team gets to know an ill person early in the illness, and, if the illness becomes terminal, offers more intensive help during the dying phase, at which point it is referred to as a "hospice team." Such a team is ideal, for it means that there will be continuity with the doctors and other medical helpers.

So when do you need these teams?

The courses of some illnesses are easier to predict than others. For example, if you are the parents of a child with a slowly worsening neurologic disorder, you are faced with a long period of uncertainty about when and how your child will die. A hospice or palliative care referral can be extremely helpful to you in this situation, to prepare and educate you and your family. They are very helpful in deciding about advance directives (see Step G). If insurance coverage is uncertain because it is unclear how long the service will be needed, ask for a one-time consultation to start you off on getting the information you will need in the future.

As has been mentioned, fear that a hospice referral means that a patient will soon die sometimes keeps doctors from suggesting, and patients and families from using, hospice providers earlier in the course of a child's disease. More than once anguished parents have asked me, "Why didn't I hear about hospice sooner?" They have realized that hospice professionals provide compassionate, family-centered care with a focus on medical symptom control as well as psychological well-being. You can request that your child's doctor remains in charge of (or at least involved with) medical decisions, so you don't lose the medical team you are used to.

Eight-year-old Tammy had metastatic cancer: Her family wanted to try experimental chemotherapy, even though the chance of cure was quite low. Though not very strong, she remained happy and playful. The chemotherapy drug had only mild side effects, and she could take it by mouth, without being in the hospital. A hospice consultation was obtained, and the hospice staff became involved during this chemotherapy. They were able to begin preparing Tammy's parents and sister for her death when it became clear a few months later that the treatment was not working. The result was that the decision to stop the chemotherapy and to stop trying to control the cancer was made at a time when there was staff available to aggressively treat pain and to help the family to handle the death at home. Everyone was grateful that when all this came about, the family had already developed a relationship with the hospice team.

If you don't feel that now is the time for referral to palliative or hospice professionals, keep this in mind for the future. It is an invaluable source for help, information, and solace that should not be underestimated.

I learned the importance of hospice from two mothers. Sally, whose son Allen died of a large tumor in his abdomen, remains tormented, years after his death, by the terrible pain her son suffered. She called her medical team's nurse many times about the pain, but was told that the doctor could not increase the dose of morphine. Yet Mary, whose daughter Leah died of the same kind of tumor, had been able to call a pain specialist at all hours of the day or night to get what her daughter needed for pain. Why, I wondered, had one child suffered needlessly while another was given the help she needed? The answer, as I was to learn again and again, was hospice and palliative care. These people come when you need them, having been there for many families, and they know what you need and what you should expect.

Consider, for example, what happened with 10-year-old David, who had a brain tumor that had spread so much that he was not expected to survive a year. David's medical team, in addition to starting chemotherapy and radiation, referred the family to the palliative care team. This team worked with David's doctors to prepare him and his family for the possibility of his death and helped them to set up a plan to treat the pain that David's tumor was causing. The family was helped by that approach; David's father said he was relieved to know they would have the help they needed no matter what happened. As it turned out, David's tumor responded to the treatment. The palliative care team stayed in the background for six months, at which point his tumor came back. Then, when he was dying, David and his family were helped by a palliative care team that they already knew and trusted. David died surrounded by loved and familiar people, not strangers. (There are more details about hospice in Step R.)

STEP I: TALKING TO YOUR FAMILY

The Adults

When your child is diagnosed with a life-threatening illness, it helps if your immediate and extended family members and close friends have a good understanding of the situation. They do not need every detail, but they need to know enough to feel comfortable and potentially be helpful to you.

At the time of initial diagnosis, when you are still stunned and your emotions are strong and mixed, you might want to organize a family meeting. That way, you don't have to keep explaining things over and over, one phone call at a time. Your child's doctor, or another representative from the medical or palliative care team, can be there to answer questions. After that, appoint one or two people to be responsible for communicating medical updates to the whole group. Doing this decreases the chance of misunderstandings about the diagnosis and treatment among your family members. They are more likely to support your decisions if they understand them.

Marilyn, whose teenage son Carl was very ill with worsening cystic fibrosis, became stressed by the many phone calls about her son's condition, loving and well-meaning though they were. She talked with her friend Blanche, who agreed that Marilyn would keep her updated, and Blanche in turn would call Carl's grandparents and other people close to the family. This took pressure off Marilyn and provided information to everyone who needed to be kept current. At the family's request, a prayer chain was also created.

This communication arrangement is even more important when your child has become terminally ill or injured and is dying. You need the support of your family and loved ones, so you have to help them understand your situation now more than ever. This can be difficult. They will all need to get past their own anger, sadness, and denial, and their emotions may initially be a drain on you. A meeting of your family and loved ones with a medical person, a chaplain/ pastoral counselor, and the social worker from the medical, palliative care, or hospice team present, is a good way to get most of the medical information communicated to the group. This setting will allow everyone's emotions to be expressed in the presence of professionals trained to handle it with you.

These meetings, and the conversations that follow, are likely to be emotionally painful and draining. People will have strong feelings about the right thing to do. Some may question the treatment decisions that you and the medical team have made. They may feel you are letting your child die or, on the other hand, prolonging his suffering unnecessarily. Some people simply cannot contain their expressions of grief. While you will need a lot of honest sharing of emotions, you may not have the energy to deal with other people's emotional needs. The staff can be very helpful here, both to deal with the immediate emotional impact of your family's reactions and to give you tools to continue to deal with them as they come up. If you have chosen hospice, the hospice staff is available to field questions and offer help.

In the midst of everyone's emotional response to your child's imminent death, remind yourself over and over that it is *your* child, and that he, you, and your medical team are in charge of the decisions. If any family members are second-guessing any of your decisions, remind yourself and them of this. Consider any useful advice or information they may have to offer—but remember that the decision is ultimately yours.

Family communication with the medical team was especially helpful in the case of Billy, a 4-year-old dying of a severe infection caused by a genetic disorder that had weakened his lungs; he was on a ventilator in the intensive care unit. His parents continued to hope for recovery even though he was desperately ill; they and the doctors decided to try an experimental medicine. Grandparents and other family members would pull the doctors and nurses aside and angrily accuse them of giving false hope; it became clear that they were saying similar things to the parents. The parents and staff arranged a meeting with the whole family, in which it was made clear that the parents needed to try this treatment in order to give Billy every chance, in spite of the likelihood that he would die. The family finally agreed to accept the parents' decision. He did die, but his parents were at peace, knowing they had left nothing undone for their boy—and they did not have to deal with painful family recriminations.

Once you have helped your family to understand your decisions, use the opportunity of these conversations to let them know what they *can* do for you. (See Step D.) When talking with your family now, it remains more important than ever to let them know what you need, and to get your needs met.

Your family members will continue to react and respond in different ways based on their individual capacity for processing extremely difficult feelings. Some will be very emotional, while others will be "stiff upper lip" types. Some will pull back, threatened by having to face such a painful reality. Among them, there will be those who eventually come to terms with their fears and give you their support at that time. But others may never deal with it at all. You can't force them to, and you have to understand that their withdrawal is because of their own problems, not yours. Use the professionals on the medical team to help all who are willing to accept that help. The more that you, or any of your loved ones, can facilitate open, honest communication, the more manageable this situation will become.

Children and Adolescents

You'll also need to talk to the children and adolescents in your family to help them understand your child's worsening medical situation. All the issues we discussed in Step E will remain true for them, and probably intensify when they realize their sibling will die. There are a number of professionals to help with this, such as Child Life Specialists, child development nurses and physicians, psychologists and other mental health workers, social workers, and spiritual counselors. If such staff are not available at your hospital, ask for help to find a good local resource person. (See Further Resources in the back of this book for help in finding assistance.) You'll want someone specially trained to work with children and adolescents of various ages to determine their unique fears and concerns and to help prevent their suffering undue alarm and psychological damage. You can have such a person present with you and the children when you talk, or you can simply ask them to give you guidance for when you have the conversations.

These children will need to be reassured that their emotions are normal. Help them by realizing that their emotional responses will vary from day to day. As far as how much to tell them, the answer varies with the child's age. It is usually safe to go as far as their questions take you, but of course it has to feel safe and permissible for them to ask. Ask them directly whether they have any questions. Then ask them what they are afraid of. This can be a difficult and sad conversation; you may want professionals to be present. One thing that teens whose siblings have gone through long illnesses have taught us is that they resent being told the truth about the illness by someone outside their family. Sometimes parents withhold information even when the sibling is dying, and these children are faced with a sudden loss they've had no time to prepare for. This may seem like a kindness—they're being spared pain for as long as possible. But it *isn't* kind: The shock of the loss is bewildering, and when they later realize—as they often do—that they have been deceived, they suffer more pain and confusion.

Nine-year-old Clara, whose sister Betty was dying from heart disease, began having serious behavior problems in school as Betty's disease worsened. Though Clara knew her sister was sick, she had not been told the extent of the illness. The medical team suggested that Clara's acting up was probably related to the ongoing stress in the family, which she couldn't understand. Her parents felt very strongly that she was not to be told the truth for fear that it would harm her. They said that Betty had pneumonia and insisted that no one tell Clara otherwise. As a result, Clara was not given help from Child Life Specialists or other preparation for the loss that was coming. This was done out of a loving, protective instinct, to keep Clara from grieving before it was necessary. But Clara knew all along that *something* was going on and was frustrated and frightened when she didn't know what it was. Betty's death came as a shock to her. She continued to have extreme school difficulties for years after Betty died. This situation probably could have been improved by more direct conversations with her.

What you choose will depend on the personalities of each of the children. Most parents feel that they should be the ones talking to their children, rather than strangers, even if those strangers are professionals. However, some children fear upsetting their parents, so they are not forthcoming about their fears and concerns. If you can, talk with the psychosocial team about what would be best for all your children.

Our culture has historically shielded children from the issues surrounding dying. This is unfortunate; children need help coming to terms with the death of a loved one, and they will do much better in the present as well as the future if they are told the truth. Honest, direct communication geared toward their level of understanding can help them to deal with this difficult reality. They will have much less trouble dealing with death for the rest of their lives if dying is not hidden from them now.

The most important children to talk with are, of course, your child's siblings. Should you tell them their brother or sister is dying? Yes, they need to know (in what detail depends upon their age), and they need the opportunity to prepare for their sibling's extended illness, and possible death. Certainly they know their sibling has been sick for a while, probably in the hospital at times. If they have not been told directly that the child may not get better, they know from the disruption and the emotions they sense around them that things are not going well. Sit down with them and tell them that their sibling is getting sicker, and see where their questions go from there. Ask them what *they* think is happening to him and lead the discussion gently from that opening.

This approach worked for the parents of Emma, a 7-year-old girl who was dying from leukemia. Emma's younger sister, Beth, had become used to a life affected by frequent trips to the clinic and the hospital. But when Emma's illness went into remission, these disruptions had stopped and the family life was happier. Then the disease came back, and Beth was angry and frustrated that life had become hard again. Her parents told her that this time the leukemia wasn't going away. Beth was distraught, convinced that her anger had made Emma's illness worse. Her parents reassured her that neither she nor anyone else had made Emma sick, and that being angry with someone could never make them ill. They told her that it was normal to feel sad and angry. They asked her if she had any questions.

"Does it hurt her?" she asked tearfully.

"A little," they said honestly. "But the doctors are giving her a good medicine that will make the pain go away."

That night at bedtime, Beth asked her mother if Emma was going to die. Yes, they said sadly, she was. Then they reminded her that Emma had had some wonderful things in her short life, and that one of them was a sister like Beth. Beth continued to ask the questions that she needed to ask, something she could do because she was made to feel that it was good and safe to ask, and to talk about it. After Emma's death she was able to express her grief. This helped her to move beyond it eventually, and incorporate it into her new normal life.

Especially with younger children, be sure to avoid evasive and confusing language, such as "going to sleep." The children may later be afraid to go to sleep themselves, thinking that they too might die. Or, they may just wait for their sibling to come back, since he should just wake up. If you believe that your child will go to heaven, it's fine to say that— as long as you make it clear that heaven is a place people don't come back from. Otherwise you risk your children expecting their sibling to come back from heaven, as he would from any other trip. If you say that the child is "going to God," you may create the similar expectation that this is a vacation and he will return from his visit with God. It is not that you should avoid comforting concepts such as these, but they need to be paired with the information that the child is indeed dying, and will not be returning.

A young child will probably be frustrated and bewildered that you and the doctors cannot fix his sibling's illness. "Fixing," after all, was the whole reason that all those trips to the hospital and clinic were made, wasn't it? And he has probably seen his parents fix many other problems. You will need to stress that everybody did their best, but that this is a problem no one could fix. Like Beth in the anecdote above, the child may think that an unkind remark he made caused his sibling to become ill. Remind him that this is not so. Find simple language to let him know what *did* cause it, because at this age his imagination may come up with something worse. Let the children be with their ill sibling as much as possible, and have a support person available for them. Have these conversations, and opportunities for questions, often.

Adolescents are harder to predict and can be more challenging. They are already in a time of great change, struggling toward personal independence. The world outside the family is at least as important to them, if not at times more so, as family life. They are intellectually able to understand illness and possible death, but at this age of feeling invincible it may not seem that this can apply to themselves or their siblings. It will be important to provide frequent opportunities for discussion and questions. Be honest and direct, and allow your older child to participate in family discussions of the medical condition. Listen to their questions, and allow the discussion to end when they need it to. They may be feeling overwhelmed. Be sure to come back to it later, and acknowledge all their emotions as normal and to be shared.

Sometimes your other children will feel that they cannot leave the ill child. This is especially true when a seriously ill child appears to be dying. If this is taking place in the hospital, it is usually possible and desirable for the whole family to be with the child during this time. If he is dying at home, of course, you yourself make all the rules. It is probably un-realistic, though, to have brothers and sisters maintain a bedside vigil when it is unclear if and when the child will die. Help them to maintain normal activities as much as possible. You can promise to call them when there is a dra-matic change in the child's condition. This obviously means that their schoolteachers need to be kept up to date as well—as they should be throughout the illness.

Nancy, a teenager whose 7-year-old sister was dying of cancer, held a vigil for a time. She had what she felt to be cherished time with Sarah, being a sort of second mother. Her family helped Nancy to return to school with the prom-ise that they would call her home immediately when needed. They called the day Sarah was dying, and Nancy held her sis-ter's hand then as she died. In the years after this, she proudly told peers in her support group how much help she had been.

Be sure to continue to work with your children's schools as their sibling's illness progresses. This is especially impor-tant at this age, as school can be an additional support for your adolescent children. Preparation can be made in ad-vance for unexpected absences, and for extra academic and psychological support when the child returns to school. School counselors can be good resources not only for your children, but also for your sick child's classmates during his illness and following his death.

Your ill child's cousins, friends, and classmates will also benefit from honest conversations about the advancing ill-ness. This should not necessarily be your burden, but sug-gest to their parents that it will be best if these children are prepared, too. They can work through their thoughts and emotions by talking, and by making cards and gifts for your ill child. They should be allowed to visit him when the situation permits. You will find that not all parents will be open to this, but if they ask, you can have Child Life and/or other team members work with them as well. Someone from the medical team may even be able to visit the school and help with this. Research on childhood bereavement tells us this is especially important: Those children who were involved in the process (visiting the dying person, helping in some way, and so on) are far more comfortable later on with the death than if the person mysteriously disappeared from their lives, leaving them no chance to say good-bye.

STEP J: GETTING COUNSELING AND SUPPORT FOR YOURSELF

You may or may not have developed a close relationship with your child's doctors and nurses. Although they have a special interest in caring for the whole family of the child who is ill, they are not trained to provide all facets of the counseling that you need in your situation. Even if you are close to the medical team, it's wise to find individual counseling support for yourself. This can be a one-time talk or a series of meetings.

Such counseling is usually best provided by those people skilled in dealing with parents of critically ill children. The social worker, psychologist, or pastoral care worker on your medical team may be helpful. You might, however, prefer to talk to someone who is not directly involved with your child's medical care. If you're already in psychotherapy, you might simply want to work on these issues with your therapist. The specific questions you can ask to find the counselor that is right for you are these:

- Where can I find someone skilled in counseling those who have faced the serious illness of a child?
- Where have other parents found helpful counseling— particularly parents of children with the same diagnosis?
- Are there any parent support groups in the area that can help me find the right people to talk to?

If the medical team cannot find a suitable counselor for you, there are other ways to find such help. Children's hospitals, clergy, and mental health agencies can give you the names of therapists.

Don't reject counseling for fear of time constraints or of being labeled as "crazy," or put it off as unnecessary. Coping with the potential loss of a child is even more traumatic without help. Working with a counselor not only helps you, but it enables you to better help your family. You and your child's other parent might also want to talk about whether to seek counseling together, or separately. You may each have different needs; different personalities deal with this type of stress quite differently, and often gender plays a part in the difference. Parents who don't face their feelings, or who have trouble keeping their feelings in control, frequently have a much more difficult time when their child's illness progresses and worsens.

You may be experiencing serious anxiety and/or depression. This makes the need for professional help even greater. There is medication and therapy that can help you to deal with these symptoms, and keep you functioning at the level that you and your family need.

Consider Karen and Tom, the parents of 3-year-old Martha, who was dying at home of a brain tumor. They sought counseling for their other children. Karen recognized that she too needed counseling and obtained this help from the medical team social worker. By contrast, Tom held back his feelings at first, and it was only two months after Martha's death that he was able to seek help. At that stage, the family entered grief counseling together. These parents later told us that each element of counseling the family obtained was invaluable in helping them face harsh situations and in caring for each other.

If you do not feel the need for professional help just now, keep it in mind for later. Try to seek out a parent support group, and remember that it is a sign of strength, not of weakness, to seek help in this difficult time. This can be difficult in our culture, especially for men. Too often we see "strength" as meaning absolute resilience. But it takes courage and wisdom to let go of that image, to embrace the strength of the flexible willow rather than the solid oak. Someone who has been through this will understand, as no one else can. As one mother told me, "When I looked into that other mother's eyes, I saw a depth of understanding I'd never experienced before." She further explained that she had felt inadequate needing such help—shouldn't a mother be able to handle anything? Instead, it turned out to be something that felt "strong."

STEP K: *TALKING WITH YOUR DYING CHILD*

You as parents love your child more than anyone else does. Especially when he was very young, your instincts helped you to know when your child needed something—a hug, or a nap, or some encouragement, or just to have you sit there quietly. You are used to protecting him, and all your instincts, and your history with him, cry out now for you to do so at this time when he needs protection more than ever. Your instincts to protect your child are very strong. How hard your inability to protect him from this illness or injury must be! Perhaps your instinct will be to protect him by hiding from him the fact that he is dying.

But you do not necessarily do him a favor by withholding the truth. You can learn how to talk to your child, and help him: There are ways to talk gently and truthfully with him without being overwhelming and destructive. But to reassure him that everything is okay, when your eyes and voice—and his own, internal wisdom—say otherwise, creates a tension in him that is anything but peaceful. Children are very insightful, and the pain in the hearts of their loved ones is obvious to them.

Further, children tend to know their bodies very well. I have had the experience several times of telling a child that his tumor is back, or his disease has progressed, only to have him say, "I know." When I pursue this, he describes not only symptoms, but also a sense that he feels as he did when he was first diagnosed. He understands that when such a bad illness returns, it is likely to be fatal. We should not fear this insight, but be grateful, impressed, and probably humbled by it. We can work with it.

Dying adults can look back on a life lived, and possibly teach the people around them about achieving peace of mind about dying. Perhaps it seems at first glance that a child, especially a very young one, has no such life lessons to offer. But this isn't the case. Zach, an 8-year-old boy I worked with who was dying of cancer, told me that he knew he was dying but didn't want me to tell his mother. "It will make her cry," he explained, more worried about her sadness than about his own upcoming death.

"How do you know that you're dying?" I asked him.

"My tummy feels just like it did when the cancer first came," he said matter-of-factly. I have heard variants of this story many times, by many different doctors and nurses, about many different children.

Some children, particularly adolescents, are old enough to do some of the same thinking that adults can do. Often they have set some life goals, and completion of these is as important for them as it would be to any adult. But they don't always talk about this to their parents or medical workers. So it is important for the adults around them to try to find out what goals such children may have, and then to help them meet those aims. These can be simple, like making a book about their life, or more complex, like graduating from college. In my experience, early diplomas have been achieved when we asked the right people!

Several teenagers I have worked with have clear priorities about their therapy because of their goals. Often they want limits set to their treatment. They may not want to live out their lives in the hospital, even if it means a few more weeks or months of life. They may want to go to school so they can graduate before they die, or complete drivers' education so that they can die as licensed drivers. One 16-year-old whom we expected would die soon clung to life for weeks, waiting for a letter. It arrived, finally—telling him he was accepted to the college he wanted to go to, and offering him a scholarship. The next day he died. He was at peace, feeling that his life was complete. This acceptance letter might seem pointless to an adult, as we tend to see such things as means to an end rather than the end itself. Why bother with a license if you won't live to drive, or a scholarship when you won't be able to use it? But for a teenager, such a goal can represent the successful conclusion to his life, proof that he has accomplished something in his short time on earth.

I've seen teenagers gather all their loved ones around them before they have died, pick out the music they want played at the time of death and at the funeral, write out their wills, and make sure their friends are okay. Sometimes this has occurred just a few days after the teenager has raged with anger at the unfairness of his fate.

Younger children can be just as amazing in their last days. They feel what is happening to their bodies, they see the looks in their parents' eyes, yet they continue to live their lives. They want to feel good today: They try to have some fun; they try to make mommy and daddy laugh. They may even try to get their siblings in trouble! They are living their lives fully, for as long as they can.

I remember 8-year-old Susan, dying at home from advanced cancer. She was on intravenous morphine, which enabled her to play comfortably most of the day with her parents and siblings. Her appetite was failing, and she was less and less able to eat. When most of us thought she would die within hours, she had a particularly important talk with her mom. Fearing that Susan felt guilty for dying and leaving them, her mother told her that it was okay for her to go to Jesus today. But Susan was having none of it—not yet. "No way, no how, not today!" she grinned. She had two more days of comfort and happy time with her family before she died, very peacefully.

In Step C, we discussed children's fears in the face of serious illness. We suggested involving mental health professionals in helping you negotiate your way through the difficult decisions called for when talking to your child about death. In determining how much to tell him about the advance of his illness, it's even more important to find a delicate way to approach this painful conversation. Telling the truth isn't as simple as saying bluntly to your child, "You are dying." It involves giving the child the opportunity to ask questions, and keeping the answers truthful. Having professionals on the medical team to help you with these conversations, or prepare you for them, can be crucial. There is no reason to allow the technology and harshness of a hospital setting to make you and your child feel totally out of control.

The child who knows on some level that he's dying may or may not be ready to face it consciously. It's important to read the signs and tell him only as much as he wants to hear. So, one approach is to demonstrate a willingness to talk, which will lead him to ask questions. You can ask about his understanding of his illness, then answer the questions as they come. Perhaps it would help to look at a few examples of young children asking their parents these questions.

Father: Is there anything you'd like to ask us?

Child: Am I going to have any more surgery or medicine?

Father: No more surgery; that's all done now. You'll keep getting medicine for the way your tummy hurts.

Child: Is the cancer back?

Father: Yes, it's back. Your mother and I are very sad about that.

Child: What's going to happen now?

Father: We're going to go home. You're going to keep getting that medicine so it doesn't hurt.

The child may finish the conversation there, or keep going. He may resume it another day, when there is a quiet time, or when there is a change in his body that brings up the question. Your honest answers will have helped him to feel safe in asking more.

Child: Mommy, am I going to die?

Mother: Yes, you are. The doctors couldn't make the cancer stay away.

Child: Will it hurt?

Mother: No, we are going to keep giving you the medicine so it doesn't hurt. And we'll do those backrubs that you like.

Child: Will I go to heaven?

Mother: Yes, you will be there with Grandpa. And Dad and I will be there with you before you know it, because in heaven, years feel like minutes! We'll miss you, but we'll be okay. You can be our angel.

Your belief system may be similar to this; even if it is not, your child's responses will guide you to voice similar reassurances that fit with your beliefs.

Knowing that he's dying allows a child to finish off the business of his life, just as it does with an adult. After talking with her parents, Jane, a 7-year-old dying from heart disease, began to make a kind of will. She listed her most precious belongings and the names of those among her family and friends that she wanted to leave them to. She was proud that she had accomplished something important. Further, she had the precious chance to say good-bye to everyone. Obviously, if no one had talked to her about what was happening, she might not have been able to do what she did for herself—and for her parents, because they now saw how at peace she was.

It's important to speak with your child as early as possible, when he is still able to communicate easily. But you may not have a chance to do this. Sometimes medical technology, sedation, or the child's overall condition will prevent him from being able to ask questions. If you learn that this will likely happen, talk to him immediately, so that he knows what to expect, and then continue talking to him afterward. One child I worked with was about to be placed on a respirator, at a time when his parents and the doctors did not know if he would live or die. His mother talked to him, explaining that when the breathing tube was in, he wouldn't be able to talk, but that she would be there with him. Her son asked how long it would be in, and she answered, honestly, that she didn't know but would tell him as soon as she did. Later, when the tube was in and the child had been on the respirator for a time, it became clear that he would die. His parents continued to talk to him reassuringly, telling him they were with him, and that he didn't have to be afraid. They continued to give him this kind of comfort until he died.

If you aren't able to tell your child what is happening before he's on the respirator, explain things to him, gently, and continue talking to him, holding his hand and touching him. Even children who are unconscious or in a coma can hear you, and can understand the reassuring tone in your voice.

Talking to older children and adolescents is similar—give honest answers to their questions. The difference is that these kids were on the verge of emancipation and independence before their illness took over, and they are likely to be more aware of what they are losing. Having a serious illness can make an older child grow up fast, and when you talk to them about illness and imminent death, it can be pretty much like talking to an adult. They will have had some life experiences to review, and some people and events to come to terms with. They may challenge you with the unfairness of what has happened to them. Again, a professional counselor can be enormously helpful.

For an adolescent, the opportunity to participate in decisions about treatment alternatives can reinforce a sense of control. He may feel that he should be permitted to make his own medical decisions, and there is a movement in pediatric medicine to give adolescents a much larger role than before. The age at which this is possible is variable, and is currently a subject of discussion in the medical field. There may come a time when your child voices an opinion about medical treatment choices that is different from yours. At these times, listen to him, and use the medical team's help in making sure that all of you are understood.

This was the situation for the parents of Frank, a 17-year-old with a cancerous tumor that had come back. His parents wanted to try an experimental medicine given in the hospital by I.V. Frank said emphatically that he didn't want to spend any more time in the hospital. This was a source of conflict for the family, and the medical team worked with them to help them to come to a mutual decision. They proceeded with the medicine, but did some of the I.V. fluids at home instead of in the hospital. Frank was an active participant in his treatment decisions from that point on.

There is no question that these conversations can become incredibly painful and emotional. Your child may be quite angry, and you may be the closest people involved, so you'll get the brunt of that anger. Use the team to help you, and be willing to stick with him through all of his emotions. Your strength—and sometimes this means willingness to show tears and weakness—and availability are important to him now. Remember that there is no one simple right answer to your decisions; you and your child together cannot get this wrong. The process of facing advanced illness and dying is complex and difficult. However, as long as you know that you tried your best for him, you will later be able to make peace with how it worked out.

Overall, your child will probably amaze you with his capacity to live with the situation. Being truthful with him allows him to proceed with living fully until death, and to try to meet his specific goals and desires. It will become your challenge to match his peaceful demeanor as he goes about what is natural to him—living one day at a time.

STEP L: FINDING OUT YOUR CHILD'S SPECIAL DESIRES AND GOALS

We have all heard about people with a life-threatening illness who "waited" to die until after a particularly special event came to pass. A son's wedding, a grandchild's birth, one's own graduation—such things sometimes keep a dying person alive longer than he might otherwise have lived. Besides major events, there are other milestones in life that are relevant. For example, a person may need to obtain forgiveness from someone he has wronged, or to express forgiveness to someone who has wronged him. Though your child is young, there might be something like this that you can help to make possible. It's important that you try to find this out. What are his hopes and desires?

Now is a good time to learn your child's thoughts about his wishes. Within the limits of his current medical condition, what would he like to see happen now? I know of a family whose dying child desperately wanted a puppy. They bought it for him, and they all enjoyed the puppy together for the last two months of his life. The dog remains a well-loved member of the family, and a living connection to their beloved son.

In pediatrics, we are fortunate to have the Make-A-Wish Foundation (MAW) and similar organizations whose mission is to bring joy to children with life-threatening illnesses. These groups provide seriously ill children with a special gift, determining what the gift will be through interviews with the child. It may be a family trip, the opportunity to meet a particular person, or an item like a computer system. This usually happens not when the child is dying but rather when the treatments are done or at a resting point, and he is strong and well enough to enjoy his wish.

But even without a formal organization such as MAW, you can fulfill your child's wish. Playing in a big chess tournament. Going to a father-daughter formal dance. Having an American Indian ceremony recognizing friendship and maturity. Writing a special piece of music. Finishing a set of paintings. These are just a few of the things children have done with their families weeks or even days before their deaths. Their sense of accomplishment and satisfaction cannot be overstated. And as their parents have witnessed these events and seen how important they were to the kids, they have felt proud even while suffering the painful knowledge that the events would soon become memories from a life cut short.

As you talk to your child about these issues, realize that he may have different ideas and priorities depending on how he is feeling day to day. This might be a gradual process as your child discovers your willingness to discuss what is on your mind and his. Be willing to ask some of the questions another day. Let him lead the conversation and, most importantly, let him express himself. Goals and wishes will likely change over time if your child's condition worsens or his level of function changes. Be open to what is important to him and try to help him meet realistic goals, one day at a time.

Chapter 5

Your Spiritual Mindset

*I prayed so hard and so long, and you know, I think I
got prayed out. I got so angry that I shook my fist at
heaven. I look back, and I remember this moment
when our Rabbi told us that was okay, that "God can
take it." He accepted my anger, and helped me out of it
at the same time. He's still helping me.*

For some parents, the diagnosis of their child's life-
threatening disease leads to spiritual questioning; this
is only magnified by the contemplation of her death.
Whether or not organized religion is a major part of your
life, you will most likely find yourself thinking about how
your child's condition and possible death fit into the view
you have of life and its meaning. In working through these
issues, with the help of a clergy member and others close to
you or on your own, you may identify unexpected resources
and sources of strength.

Spirituality involves a belief that we are all connected to a
greater power. Being spiritual does not necessarily mean

a belief in a particular religion, or even a particular definition of God. Most organized religions do have, along with a
belief in a higher power, a belief that the soul will live on. If
you do have such beliefs, they can be a great source of comfort to you now.

STEP M: *EXAMINING SPIRITUAL VIEWS ON LIVING AND DYING*

Adults who are dying may turn to their spiritual beliefs to
envision a life beyond this one. Their journey to peace may
involve thinking about their dying, to put it in the context of
the passing from this life to the next. However, when the
passage is not your own but your child's, it can be much
more difficult.

Examining your spiritual beliefs can help you to coexist
with suffering without being overwhelmed by it. It can help
you to differentiate your various emotions, distinguishing
what is useful from what is unproductive; it can help you
open up to others, asking for their thoughts on what's happening and evaluating their input rationally. Your belief
about the world and what it offers, your belief about a
higher power or what is meaningful in your life: These affect
the way you cope with any situation, including the agony of
losing a beloved child.

The issues surrounding death and dying are rarely separa-
ble from spirituality. Thus, the parents of a dying child frequently find themselves asking, "Is there a purpose to my

child's suffering and the struggle our family is having?" "How can my child be dying when she hasn't even had a chance to live?" "What is the nature of the next phase of my child's existence?" "How can there be any higher power or God when this horrible thing is allowed to happen?" You may find your faith hazy or you may be struggling with a loosened spiritual foundation as you face your child's potential death.

If these questions are on your mind now, dealing with them is important. The thought processes involved, and ultimately the answers you find, will depend heavily on your belief systems. Take some time to think about just what those are. Perhaps this ordeal has brought you back to a spiritual upbringing that you had left behind, or that just wasn't at the forefront of your adult life. Or, your child's condition may have brought you to spiritual resources for the first time. Try to keep an open mind about these resources.

At the beginning, though, you may feel betrayed by a spiritual life that has previously been a comfort. Letting the reality of your child's impending death into your thoughts may be too hard.

Too hard, that is, without help. That help can come from trained professionals (more on that later); it can also come from the child herself. Children have sometimes described angels that have appeared to them. Sometimes they tell of a conversation with a family member who has already died. Or they dream of dead family members, understanding the dream as a kind of visit in which the beloved person is promising a happy reunion. Parents who are open to hearing what their child has to say at this time receive a real gift—sometimes a guide to knowing that the child will be all right after death. Sally, the 5-year-old daughter of a single mother, dreamed frequently about angels and woke her mother nightly asking, "Can't you see them, Mom?" Finally one night she woke her mother and said, "Mommy, there are two angels here. One is for you and one is for me. Mine will make sure I'm all right and let you know, and yours will do the same for me." She died peacefully early that morning, having given her mother the gift of protection and of the knowledge that neither of them would be alone.

The meaning that parents come to find in their child's death will be unique to each family. When children are well, people who are paying attention can learn much from them. Just as seeing life "through the eyes of a child" can help adults achieve wisdom, so too can a child's dying be instructive. I was fortunate to be part of a team working with 7-year-old Pedro when he died. His family and the medical staff surrounded him as he lay quietly, his hand in his mother's. Suddenly he sat up and looked in front of her, his eyes full of joy and wonder. He said nothing; he simply lay back down and died peacefully. At first no one spoke. Then, almost embarrassed, someone whispered, "He saw heaven!" We all nodded; we all believed it. If adults could achieve the wonder and peace and acceptance seen in that dying child, we might find meaning and comfort to last the rest of our lives.

Sometimes parents come to spiritual understanding on their own or simultaneously with the child. The dying process can produce in people a common spirituality, one that may not be associated with a particular religion. It involves seeing the necessity of love, forgiveness, kindness, honest communication at times of crisis, and being open to the experience, even in the face of the unthinkable. The families for whom this happens are the ones who find meaning and peace, serenity and comfort, even as they enter a time of intense grieving.

Joan, the mother of a 5-year-old boy who died at home of advanced cancer, explained this experience to me very clearly. She and her partner, Marla, had been faced with many hard decisions when their child's disease relapsed. They felt that the work they did gathering information, trying to understand it, and making decisions after that was their way of being good parents, given "what life had thrown at us, for us to do with God's help." Joan explained that she felt at peace because she knew she couldn't have done anything differently: She had done a good job, and had been a "good mom." Emphatically, she said this didn't mean she felt "at peace" with her boy's death. She meant simply that as she grieved her son, she didn't have to struggle with thinking "if only," or torture herself with the fear that she'd made any wrong decisions. She had put it in God's hands, she told me.

There are, of course, many different cultures, many different belief systems about death, and many individual beliefs. There is no one right way of thinking or finding meaning in this situation. Those who believe in heaven can be comforted by the certainty that their child is there, happy and no longer suffering. One family I learned of talked about their belief in reincarnation: They were certain that these young souls would move on to the next human lifetime, this short life having taught them the lessons that they were supposed to learn. They felt that the lives of children who died young were "filler lives" chosen by these souls, knowing that they would cause an enormous amount of pain for these parents. Through this pain, they believed they were to learn about the nature of love. As harsh as that may seem, the parents were at peace with this.

Even without a belief in the afterlife, there can be comfort in the memory of your child, and in the knowledge that, like the mother we spoke of earlier, you have done everything possible for her. Because of your courage and persistence, she suffered less than she might have; you made the little time she had to live precious to her.

Finding meaning in the death of a child may also happen at some point after the child has died. Parents and others learn lessons that can enrich their lives and in turn offer them strength at the time of their own dying. This is not easy to see while grief and loss are all-consuming. It usually takes time to see what growth has occurred as a result of parenting a child through dying.

A Higher Power?

The parents I have worked with who believed in a higher power have been amazingly strong. They have said to me such things as, "Our child was given to us by God, and we put her in His hands." Throughout the child's illness, they derived a sense of peace from that faith. Often the family's church has begun a prayer chain for the ill child. (In such a case, people initially pray for the child to be cured, and the parents to be comforted. Later, if it becomes clear that there is no hope for cure, they pray that the child will die peacefully and that her loved ones will be able to accept what is happening.) As I watch these parents remain strong in their faith, I long to give that sense of peace to the parents of some of my other patients.

But the spiritual questioning is not always peaceful—at least in the beginning. It is not an easy process. You may be angry with God, asking why your child's illness and death are happening. Your child's innocence, in stark contrast to the state of the adult world, may fuel your sense of unfairness and anger at God. Or you may feel God is punishing you for past sins. Your religious community may be making it harder by expecting too much of you. They may have unrealistic expectations or teachings about healing, and this can create a sense of guilt or inadequacy. I have seen one hospital chaplain help parents through this, telling them that God understands their anger, is forgiving, and is ready with comfort when they are ready to be comforted. He has taught them that anger with God is not a sin that needs forgiving, but rather a process that needs to be explored. So be patient with yourself. You do not have to be spiritually perfect. But use the resources available to you to help you sort these things out.

Your child may need these resources as well. The hospital chaplain or a church youth group leader, among others, can help her with spiritual questions that she may have. And don't forget your other children; share with them the insights you gain as you think about these issues. They may find this particularly reassuring.

Your spiritual beliefs may not include a specific God. Some systems, like traditional Native American beliefs, speak of "Spirit," which isn't envisioned as a specifically human "father," and others see divinity as existing in all living things. You don't need to adopt any one religion's beliefs; simply look to what you yourself believe.

The Question of Life After Death

Many of the parents I have worked with have found great solace in their belief that their child would continue to live on after this life. For some this life continues in heaven; for others it is less clearly defined. In any case, it can be very comforting to perceive your child at peace, happy and pain-free.

The concept sometimes goes further, to include the involvement of loved ones who have died before. Parents find consolation in the vision of their child being reunited with these people. They often believe that these souls will usher her into her new life. And they are deeply comforted by the conviction that they themselves will ultimately join their child there.

Children often have these convictions as well, and as they draw closer to death, many have profound experiences of connection with their next life. I have seen a number of children present their parents with pictures of heaven that they have drawn. One 4-year-old showed his drawing to his parents and pointed to a figure in the drawing. "That's Grandpa," he said happily. "I'm going to be with him soon." His parents were deeply moved by their son's eloquent demonstration of his peace of mind, and his certainty of where he would soon be.

A Few Suggestions

You may not be nearly as certain about these things as that child was. There is no mistaking, though, how useful it can be for you to settle some of these issues for yourselves.

So, to that end, consider giving spiritual issues more thought than you might otherwise. If you're skeptical, put that aside momentarily, and consider that you and your child might be helped in a way that you had not thought about before. Talk to the hospital chaplain or another clergy member, and see if you find yourself willing to explore some spiritual beliefs. If this doesn't appeal to you, you might want to search out someone from another tradition—perhaps a Buddhist priest or a Native American medicine man or woman.

Begin to think back on the role of spirituality in your own life so far. Is there a religion or spiritual belief you now follow? If not, and you grew up in a particular religion, it would be logical to start there. Examine what you were taught or raised with; find what is useful and keep it. If that one does not suit you, look to other belief systems. It could be that the *way* you were taught these things as a child did not offer much to you. Look deeper into the teachings of that or other faiths. Explore your beliefs and those of others—find what is true in your spirit. What do you find about living and dying? Where do you find a sense of peace, even in the face of the unthinkable? Rely on your instincts and internal barometer. You don't have to accept traditional answers, but there may be a place where you will find a sense of equilibrium.

You may find that no single spiritual belief system works for you. Different elements of Judaism, Christianity, Buddhism, Native American religions, and others might make sense to you, offer meaningful insights, and be a source of comfort.

There are people to help you with this. Parents who have already suffered the loss of children may be particularly helpful. Don't hesitate to ask them how their view of spirituality unfolded. Also, give other pastoral care workers an opportunity if the one you are working with doesn't gel with you. Different people have different ways of viewing or explaining things, and while no answers are readily available for why this is happening, there are places where you might find a sense of peace to sustain you, if you keep looking.

Many people find that they don't need an organized religion or spiritual group: They have their own sense of something larger than this life, and are able to draw on that for comfort. If you are one of these people, respect that in yourself, and allow your belief to offer you hope and comfort.

❧ Chapter 6 ❧

The Turning Point

I kept hoping he'd wake up. People have recovered from head injuries like his. But as I sat by his bed, I knew I would do whatever was best for him. I hoped for him to get better, and I hoped for him not to hurt, all at the same time. I know I never let him hurt.

Your worst nightmare has come true. The doctors have told you—or perhaps you yourself have sensed—that your child clearly will not survive.

It is normal for you to be terrified and lost—to go from pounding your fists and screaming "It's not true" to quiet acceptance, or numbness, and back again. Earlier, when you were told he *might* die, you could cling to the hope that he wouldn't. What is left to hope for now?

To begin with, you can hope for your child's comfort, today. Don't give up hope that keeps you going—the hope for a miracle cure—but keep his comfort as your major goal each time a decision has to be made.

There are hard questions you will now find yourself asking, like the ones the mother of a 9-year-old who had died of leukemia asked: "Why didn't anyone tell me it could happen like this?" The more prepared you are, the more torment you'll be spared. One father cried in anguish to me, "Why didn't you tell me he'd turn blue?" Others have wanted to know why they didn't get a hospice referral sooner, or why no one called to see how they were doing. One of the harshest questions I ever had to answer was posed by the mother of a 6-year-old who died after a long time in intensive care: "Why did you let her suffer so much?"

Parents have also asked, "Why are you asking me to decide whether to turn off my baby's ventilator?" "What will happen if we don't stop the ventilator?" someone will say, then add, "What will happen if we do? Do you realize how hard this choice is?" Many, agonized by the child's pain, ask about more morphine, or about possible other treatments for pain. "Who will help me with my other children?" is another common question. Often, they fear the doctor's disapproval: Will we become angry with them if they don't take our advice? And they long, desperately, to make sense of the unthinkable. I can still hear the voice of one despairing father: "How can I hope twenty percent?"

In this chapter, we consider the issues that will help you talk to your doctors and your family, now that things are not getting better. How can you deal with the fact that your child is more likely to die than to survive? The first step is comfort: the control of physical symptoms.

STEP N: Achieving Good Symptom Control

To begin with, as we discussed previously, it is important to ask again what the goals of treatment are now that things have changed, and what the realistic chances are of a treatment having the desired effect. As the disease progresses, the goals and types of treatments that will help meet the goals should change, too.

Over the course of your child's medical condition, you have probably used many different kinds of treatments, each with its own goal. Some of the treatments were directed toward beating the disease. Others were directed toward some of its symptoms (for example, wheezing from a lung or heart disease, fluid retention from kidney disease, pain from a tumor). Still others were directed at side effects from the treatments themselves (nausea from chemotherapy).

Your child will not be cured and is likely to die soon. *It is time to focus on treatments that will make him more comfortable in the time he has remaining.* Treatments now should be aimed at symptom control and at keeping your child comfortable, free of fear and anxiety, and as pain-free as possible. These kinds of treatments must now come first, and come whenever and wherever needed. This is referred to as "comfort-based" or "supportive" care, the medical specialty called *palliative care.* (This was discussed in Step H.)

In making such care a priority, you may continue to use some of the same treatments that you were previously using in trying to control the primary disease. For example, sometimes cancer chemotherapy or radiation reduce tumor-induced pain. But their function has now changed: They are no longer being used as curative measures, but as palliative ones. This is how it was for the family of Evelyn, an 11-year-old with an abdominal tumor that had spread to her brain. It was clear that she couldn't be cured, and the family had decided against experimental treatments. They talked with the doctors about giving Evelyn radiation therapy to shrink the tumor in her brain. The goal of this now was to relieve pain, not to cure the disease. This treatment, combined with pain medicine, helped make Evelyn more comfortable, helping her to die peacefully.

Sometimes, it is just too hard to stop trying to cure your child. No one can quarrel with that—in very rare cases, miracle cures do occur. But try, with the doctors, to keep your child's comfort (physical *and* psychological) as the top priority at this time. As before, compare the burden (side effects, hospital time) of treatment aimed at curing the disease to the likelihood of its benefit. Try not to let the curative treatment get in the way of meeting other goals your child may have, such as going to school (even just one more day or hour) or spending time with loved ones.

Getting Pain and Symptom Control

Not all doctors have good palliative care skills, for this is not currently well taught in medical schools and residency programs. As we discussed in Step H, there are pain-control and palliative-care specialists available for consultation, so you can ask your doctor to connect you with these resources. Palliative, comfort-based care should be integrated throughout the entire treatment course of advanced illness for every affected child, whether he is in the hospital or at home.

No matter where your child will die, close attention to controlling his pain and any other serious symptoms needs to be a top priority. In order for this to happen, there must be a clear plan for the continuous reevaluation of his comfort level.

It is most important that you sit down with the medical team and make a detailed plan for pain and symptom control. A team approach will work out the best. You will need to know who from the team will make assessments of your child's comfort level. Will it be you? The home care or hospice nurses? The doctors on the team? Physicians-in-training? You must find out who on the team decides what medicines to use, and what changes in medication and doses are necessary over time. You need a plan for all hours of the day or night. Will your child's primary physician decide? Who will be responsible when that person is not available? Is that backup person experienced in this area? If your child is being cared for at home and intravenous medicines are being used, what should be done if the I.V. line stops working?

These are the questions you need to ask. You may have to lobby for adequate *and timely* pain control for your child. Do not take "no" or "later" for an answer. Some home care nursing agencies that are not formal hospice services tend to have difficulty generating a timely and appropriate response. Most of their other home care patients have needs that don't require an immediate action, so they may not be used to responding very fast. But when the issue is pain control, you will need them to act at once. So if your child's situation calls for it, be demanding. Use your family members to help you be a strong advocate for your child. You will find that the hospice nurses are excellent partners for you in this.

Most likely, your child's doctor will recommend a combination of narcotic (also called opioid) and nonnarcotic pain medications. (Morphine is an example of the former, Tylenol of the latter.) This type of combination is effective for most patients, and the children are most often able to be awake and alert even at high doses. The fear of addiction to opioids is an outdated and irrelevant concept when they are used for pain control. When used to treat pain, rather than to get "high," opioids are not addictive. Please do not withhold these very effective medications from your child because of such concerns.

Opioids have side effects that must be controlled. These may include sedation, nausea, itching, or, rarely, hallucinations. Constipation *must* be prevented, with routine medication. At times, the combination of medications used for pain may cause drowsiness. Work with the doctors to determine what is tolerable given your child's condition and prognosis. You may decide that a certain level of sleepiness is tolerable. Sometimes the addition of a stimulant medication is considered. With opioid pain medicine, doses may need to be increased over time.

Dylan's doctors prescribed morphine to control the pain from his bone cancer, and it made a striking difference. The 13-year-old went from being perpetually quiet, subdued, and bedridden to being actively interested in what was going on, and he was able to participate in family activities for a few hours each day. His parents were relieved at both his comfort level and his ability to enjoy time with them.

Other medications, such as steroids, may be recommended for pain in addition to the opioids. Or a gentle sedative may add just enough relaxation to control your child's pain. He may also benefit from some other methods of pain control. This may involve procedures like a nerve block or an epidural (spinal area) catheter placement. It may involve visualization techniques, hypnosis, imagery, and/or massage.

Jane, a 10-year-old with severe leukemia, had leg pain that was only partially relieved by morphine. She was fairly anxious as well. Her parents and the medical team were both impressed and humbled when she solved her own pain and anxiety problem. She recalled how well imagery and relaxation techniques had helped her to get through spinal taps while she was in the clinic, so she used this approach in her current situation. She could do so whenever she needed, and it helped everyone's ability to cope with the illness.

The basic concept that is crucial to your child's well-being is that you and the medical team should aggressively and creatively work to maintain his comfort. The specialty of palliative medicine has come a long way in finding many different options for people in pain. Some of these options just have not found their way into routine medical care, or indeed training, yet. So, it is important for you to know that they exist, and that you can access them for your child.

Now, at this turning point in your child's treatment, you are probably experiencing a sense of defeat. You may be frustrated because you feel there is nothing you can do for him. But there is still very much to do. You have not failed because you have redefined your goals. You will not save your child's life, but you will make his last weeks or days comfortable, and help him to die peacefully. That is no small accomplishment, and it is something to be proud of.

🙿

STEP O: *Being "Ready"*

As we discussed earlier, dying children, like dying adults, can reach acceptance and readiness partly by tuning in to the changes they feel in their bodies and minds. Your child is probably tuning in to these changes as well, depending on his age and medical condition. So he may understand and accept (perhaps only subconsciously) the fact that he's dying.

But how can *you* accept it? You are not feeling what your child is feeling. Perhaps you have watched him rally from a medical crisis before, and find it hard to believe that he won't make it through this one. Your hope for your child's survival can be very hard to let go. How could a parent feel any other way?

And yet, you have to let go. For your child's sake and your own, you must prepare as much as possible for his death. You are probably saying—have said many times—"I can't do this." Now you need to change the sentence: "I can't do it *alone.*" Accept the fact that you will need help to get through the days that are coming.

It is time to prepare for change. Your hopes are no longer focused on cure. You will begin to hope instead that your child will achieve his special desires. You will begin to hope for relief of pain, for a good day today and tomorrow, for your extended family to come to terms with the upcoming death.

The story of 6-year-old Beth comes to mind. Her parents were still reeling from the news that her cancer had returned, when she began to worsen quickly. After long hours of talking with the medical team, they decided not to use any treatment that involved painful side effects, or that would have to be given in the hospital. The family concentrated on having good days, and they had some wonderful time together. As the days went by and Beth got sicker, Randy, her mother, accepted the fact that her daughter would die. Her father, Paul, however, did not. Instead, he bounced back and forth: One day he was resigned; the next he was asking about more curative treatments. This, it turned out, was his own way of preparing. Both were able to hold Beth and tell her of their love as she died peacefully. Later, they told me that while no parent could ever really be ready for their child to die, they both became as prepared as they could, in their different ways.

Paul's way of preparing for her death was no less "reasonable" than Randy's. If you prepare as he did, after many conversations with the doctors and with the people who support you, your conflicted feelings will occur less and less.

Try to set your goals of comfort-care as the top priority, along with spending good days together as a family. These days may be bittersweet, with each hour of pain-free play, each laugh, each moment of quiet intimacy cherished, while nights may be filled with tears. Some days will be up, some days down, but you can bring to each one a vow to make the best of it.

Talking to the medical team (see Step N) about putting your child's comfort first is a crucial step in readying your heart for his death. This is a most profound turning point in your life as his parent. If you are able, from this moment on, try to see your child's death as a natural consequence of his medical condition, not as some sort of failure on your part. Think of it as an inevitable part of his living, not as something to continue fighting against. Your job now is to let go of the grasping for cures, and to focus on your child as he is today.

If you achieve this level of "readiness," you can proceed with some steps to help him die peacefully. You can work toward saying good-byes, and helping the rest of your family to do so, too. You can find a serenity that contributes to his own tranquility. Serenity does not mean that you never get angry again: You will. It does not mean that the death of your child is in any way a good thing. It means simply that you have accepted the job of getting ready to do your best for your child in the time he has left.

You *can* do this, and you will *not* have to do it alone.

STEP P: KEEPING ELEMENTS OF NORMAL CHILDHOOD

One of the nicest things you can do for your child, for your other children, and for yourselves is to try to maintain some normal family life, some uplifting family- and/or child-oriented activities. This idea may run counter to how you are feeling now, and in an odd way it may feel disrespectful, as if you are minimizing what he is going through. But it isn't—it's the best way to honor him—giving him all the happiness he can have in the time he has left.

It is especially helpful to have children close to your child's age come to visit him. They can read to him, watch videos, or sit at the bedside and look at card collections or blow bubbles. They need not spend a great deal of time, but they will be a welcome diversion. It may surprise you how much it will seem to energize your child for a time. Obviously, having the parents of these friends involved and well-informed will be useful. This is something they can do for you. Perhaps your child's schoolteacher can stop by as well.

Maria was a 7-year-old who was dying in the hospital from rapidly worsening leukemia. She was very weak and needed constant medicine for pain. Unable to get out of bed for very long, she enjoyed being read to and watching videos. There were many adult family visitors, but they seemed to tire her out quickly. Then one morning, she was told that a close friend her own age was coming to visit that afternoon. When the friend arrived, Maria literally leaped out of bed and exclaimed, "I've been waiting for you!" They played with more energy than anyone thought Maria had left in her. She was tired after a few hours of that, but relaxed and happy. More visits from her friends (who had been prepared, and whose parents were there to support them) followed, cheering Maria immensely.

When your child can no longer participate actively, you can still provide him with more mild diversions. Surround him with the items and pictures that represent his favorite activities. I remember a boy who always loved to put together model cars, and the pleasure he got from watching his mother and sister build them at his bedside when he could no longer do this. It became a time of happy chatter while the building went on, and the model cars remain with the family, a warm memory of the good times they shared with little Bobby.

Your other children need to maintain their normal activities as well. Depending on their age, they will need more or less of your help and time to do this. The support of family and friends who spend time getting your children to their activities can be invaluable. Your older children may feel like they shouldn't do these things, thinking they should remain with their ill or injured sibling. Gently help them to continue at least some of their normal activities at this time. Promise to call them home or to the hospital when they are needed.

Sometimes these children may overextend themselves with outside activities. This may be a way to avoid facing the heartbreak of seeing their sibling dying, and it's a very normal way for young children and adolescents to cope. You may feel frustrated, because it takes energy that you don't have to try to deal with this. Talk to the child psychology, Child Life, or social work staff or pastoral counselor about this. They can help you understand what normal grief looks like in children. They will probably have some useful suggestions, including checking with the children's school-teachers, scout leaders, or activity coaches.

STEP Q: ENSURING THE SUPPORT OF FAMILY AND FRIENDS AS YOUR CHILD IS DYING

From this moment on, you will need some of your family and friends alongside you, even more than before. Some people will be better at this than others. Remember that facing your child's dying is hard for them, too. Sometimes people will avoid you because your situation terrifies them, reminding them that they and their own children are mortal. Let them go: Governed by such fears, they can do you little good. But others may avoid being around because they don't know what to do or say. These people are worth pursuing. To some extent, because you and this experience are unique, you have to let others know what you need. They cannot always know instinctively.

There will be some among your family and friends who remain distinctly uncomfortable with the issue of death, especially the death of a child. Their visits may be brief, and possibly unpleasant because of their discomfort. Some may stop coming altogether, and you may feel disappointment or anger because it seems like abandonment. Try to accept this and put it out of your mind. Still others may talk constantly, again because of their uneasiness. You have a right to limit visits, and you have a right to retain your privacy as you desire. You can help yourself by having a good support person with you during visiting times, one who will be strong enough to state time limits for visits, and to let people know if you and/or your child are not up to having visitors.

Your own parents may have a particularly hard time. They are facing both the loss of a grandchild and the agony that you, their own child, are suffering. In their zeal to help you, they, like others, may get stuck in their hope for your child's survival, even after you have seen that his approaching death is inevitable. Remember to involve family and close friends in the meetings with the medical team, especially those who are crucial support people. Getting them to understand the medical decisions you have made is a particularly important goal now. Your energy will be drained, and the focus taken away from the needs of your dying child, if there is conflict over decisions you have made as parents, or if there is poor communication among the people that you count on for help.

Those who can't come to understand the medical decisions you have made for your child can still support you. Use the social workers, pastoral counselors, and other medical or hospice team support staff to help you to talk with them about that, if necessary. They need to reach an acceptance that you have made the decision you believe best, and to join with you to help your child die peacefully.

This worked wonderfully for the family of Troy, a teenager who was in intensive care for several weeks following complicated heart surgery. Difficult decisions had to be made about more surgery, and members of the extended family disagreed about the decisions that this boy and his parents had made. There were hard days of uncertainty, and the family's household was pretty chaotic. The grandparents, aunts, and uncles who had been making the boy's parents feel that they were giving up too soon participated in a family meeting with the doctors. This helped them to understand that the decisions had been made with a great deal of thought. They realized that they didn't have to agree with Troy's parents, just support them. Soon these people who had been putting unwarranted pressure on the boy's parents became the group organizing help for them. Lists of who would prepare meals, who would do household chores, and who would drive the other kids to school appeared. It was a tremendous relief to Troy's parents and siblings, and it gave the relatives a legitimate sense that they were doing something to help the child they all loved. When Troy died, the family peacefully pulled together in love and support.

As we discussed in Step D, you might want to try appointing someone (or, as in the case of Troy, a group of people) to organize those who want to support you. This will help to prevent the situation in which people say, "Let me know if there is anything I can do," leaving their choice of task up to you. You may not have the energy or the desire to make individual assignments.

As important as support from your family and friends is, it's even more crucial for those of you in a two-parent household to be supportive of one another. You are in a period of anticipatory grief. People often grieve differently—frequently along gender lines. Sometimes one parent will ask the other, "Why are you okay?" when it's simply a different way of dealing with grief. One parent can begin to blame the other for causing the child's illness, for not tending to aspects of care, or for many of the other problems that can arise. Be good to one another now, and allow for a wide range of emotional responses. Use the professional staff to help you to do this. Again, this is something that you are doing for your child, because in taking care of yourselves, you make yourselves better able to take care of him.

Your situation may involve divorce or estrangement. Though it can be hard to make important medical decisions together if your relationship is strained, it can be done. The death of one adolescent boy with leukemia illustrates this. Jim's parents were going through a bitter divorce throughout his treatment. When he relapsed, they moved back in together to deal with the rigors of treatment, clinic visits, hospitalizations, and the needs of his younger brother. His father lived in the basement of the family home while his mother stayed upstairs. When Jim's illness became critical and it was clear that he would probably die, they banded together to discuss all medical decisions, to be with their dying son, and to comfort the rest of the family, including their other son, Sam. In the moment after his death, this mother and father embraced and clung to each other—not as husband and wife, but as parents. Each had lost the child, and only the other knew how that felt. Everyone involved was impressed with their ability to put their own issues selflessly aside and surround their dying son, and their living one, with united comfort. Jim's last experience was of his parents together, helping him die peacefully. And Sam understood that, though his parents would continue living apart, they would always be united in loving and caring for him as well.

CHAPTER 7

SOME NEEDED PREPARATION

I wish someone would have told me what the signs of dying were, that it was very close, what to expect, and what the physical changes meant. I think it would have been better for us, to get through those last days and hours.

*T*his will be another difficult chapter. It discusses information and issues that are emotionally difficult, but crucial if you are to make the decisions you need to make. Parents who have lost children have told us that what follows is what they wish they would have known at the time.

This is especially true of Step S, which discusses the physical changes your dying child may go through. Parents told us how terribly hard it had been to be unprepared for these changes. If you find yourself unable to read it now, put it aside until the time comes. When you need it, it will be here for you. However, when the time *does* come, please read this chapter. For your child's sake, and ultimately for your own peace of mind, it will help enormously if you are prepared for what happens, and act accordingly.

✿

STEP R: *DECIDING WHERE YOUR CHILD WILL DIE*

One of the most important decisions parents face is whether to have their child die at home or in an institution (most likely the hospital, but possibly an inpatient hospice unit if one is available). Your choice will depend on many things, the most important being your child's medical condition and the resources available to you. It is useful to learn about the choices ahead of time, so that you can thoroughly consider the pros and cons of each.

The thought of your child dying in your home is an emotional one. It can feel comforting to think about tending to your child "where she belongs," rather than in the alien environment of a hospital. On the other hand, it can feel reassuring to think about having the nurses and doctors who know her on hand to deal with her medical and comfort needs. It is normal to feel torn between your home, where her loved ones are, and the hospital, where her medical helpers are. It's important now to sort out all the issues—practical and emotional—and to consider what will be best for you and your child.

If there is an undetermined length of time from now until your child's condition changes and she is at the point of imminent death, this time can probably be spent at home, especially if the doctors think it will be weeks to months before she dies. It's a good idea to have a hospice referral, which will give you the best preparation for important medical and psychological issues. The hospice team will provide skilled help and advice in the care of your child, let you know what you can expect to happen as illness progresses, and help you to feel confident that you are doing your best to keep her comfortable.

Most people on the medical team will probably feel that the best place for your child to die is at home because they believe that bereaved parents and siblings will suffer less after the child's death. But this is not always true. Having a child die at home isn't right for all families. Over the next decade we will most likely see the medical community doing more research into this, but in any case, it will always be an individual situation. You have to decide what you think is best for you and your family.

Your feelings about your child dying in the hospital will depend in part on the kind of experiences she and the family had while she was hospitalized. Hospitals for the most part have an institutional quality, with visiting rules (restricted hours, number of people at one time), rather bland food, and limitations on your privacy. But the positive aspects include the 24-hour availability of nursing and medical staff, social workers, pastoral counselors and Child Life staff, medical equipment and monitors, and medicines.

You may be particularly hesitant to have your child die at home if you are worried that the house will become a fearful or sad place for your family to live. You may be concerned about your other children seeing their sibling die. While research has shown that sibling bereavement is less difficult when siblings are involved with the death in some way, you might feel that it is better to have that involvement take place in another environment. Or, you may add up the burdens of the medical caregiving and decide that there simply aren't enough people with enough time to devote to it. The decision is highly individual, varying from family to family. As with all of these critical decisions, there is no one right or wrong way.

Having Your Child Die in the Hospital

When you decide that your child will die in the hospital, or if there is no choice in this, you'll need to find the best way to make the hospital situation work for your child and your family.

Start with the institutional appearance of the hospital. Work with the health care team to make the hospital room as homelike as possible, with pictures and posters, children's artwork, special blankets, music, soft lighting, and anything from home that your child would want around her. She may, for example, be able to wear her own pajamas or clothing. The key is to achieve a peaceful, private, homelike environment with family and friends present.

Next, think about your role as parents, and whether there is anything about your child's care here that you can do instead of, or along with, the hospital staff. You can tend to your child as much as possible: Work with the nurses to divide some of the tasks. In doing this, you are making the situation as homelike as you can, and you are enhancing your caregiving role.

Next, ask whether some of the monitors and lab tests can be eliminated; they may have been routinely continued even though the goals of medical care have changed. Doctors and nurses are trained to perform diagnostic tests with almost any medical problem that arises. With each test, ask if it will result in improving your child's comfort. If it won't, request that it not be done. Work with the staff to eliminate rules that applied earlier, but are not relevant now, like precautions taken to prevent your child getting an infection (wearing masks, limiting the number of visitors). You may run into some people who are inflexible about this, but when you do, consult someone in a supervisory role. Don't give up on this; talk to the doctors if you need to. It is your right to make this experience as peaceful as possible.

Although you won't have to handle medical cares as you would at home, it will be most helpful to know what to expect as your child's bodily functions slow down. (We discuss this in Step S.)

Even if your child's medical condition has worsened rapidly and you have little time to prepare, you can take some of the steps we've just covered to make your situation more homelike. These things don't take a lot of time, but they do take some assertiveness. This is where your friends and family can help you. Delegate the tasks of going to get that special quilt, and music, and pictures. Try to make arrangements for a visit with a cherished pet, if at all possible. Involve your other children as much as you can.

Mark was a 14-year-old dying from lung disease. His family had a difficult time deciding whether to have him at home or in the hospital. They felt pressure from both the medical team and their extended family to be home. Over two days, the parents changed their minds several times, often feeling different from one another. Ultimately they decided to keep him in the hospital, and this decision brought relief. They went from constant worry about the right decision, to moving on firmly with the job of helping their son die well. They were able to have a big family gathering in the hospital, playing music that Mark loved, talking with him and with each other, just before he died. His sister planned the music both for this gathering and for the funeral.

Having Your Child Die at Home

To make this alternative work well, there must be one or two primary caregivers. (Usually this will be one of the child's parents.) But the primary caregiver can't do it alone, and will need additional help in the home. That need will increase as time goes on. The best kind of help comes from a hospice program (see Step H), which has a team of home care nurses, social workers, pharmacists, chaplains, and volunteers. Their resources may also include art and music therapists, nursing assistants, and bereavement specialists. The hospice team works with your child's primary doctor to provide care as her changing condition dictates. It is sometimes stressful for parents to think about bringing strangers into the situation; they want staff that the child is familiar with to help them. This is why getting palliative care and hospice staff involved early can be helpful. However, if you haven't done so earlier, you can certainly begin now.

Keep in mind that the available hospice services vary around the country. You will need to find out what resources there are in your community, and what level of experience they have with children. You can also ask about the availability of respite care: This means that your child can be admitted to a facility for one or several days so that you get needed rest (the amount of time varies according to local resources or policy).

During the initial consultation with a hospice team, an intake nurse will meet with the family to learn about your child and her unique situation; this nurse will already have received medical information from the doctors. An assessment of what is necessary to have the child cared for at home will be made. For example, you may or may not need equipment such as a hospital bed, oxygen, commodes, disposable bedding, bandages, or a wheelchair or walker. You will discuss what kind of staff help you might need, such as a nurse or home health aide for a certain number of hours each day (depending not only on your child's condition, but also on insurance coverage). The hospice service, and your child's doctor, will notify the local authorities and emergency responders of an expected death at home.

Most importantly, the hospice staff remains available to you, your child, and your family, as needed, from the time of the initial consultation until your child dies, and even afterward. You can phone them to talk about concerns, or you can have someone come to your home even outside of regularly scheduled visits. For example, you may feel that your child needs a change in medication for pain, or constipation, or another symptom. A nurse can speak with you on the phone about this, or can come to your home to help make the evaluation. A call is then made to the doctor, and a new plan can be made from there. Similarly, the staff is available for help with social or spiritual issues as well.

Hospice services vary in the amount of experience their staff has had with dying children. Some medical teams have to rely on home care nursing agencies that are not primarily hospice organizations. Be certain to ask whether the recommended hospice or home care service has had pediatric experience. This is most important in terms of the nurses who will come to your home to check on you and your child; it is best if they have experience with the evaluation and management of the problems that children have at the end of life. When they have such experience, or access by phone to such expertise, hospice nurses can be an invaluable help to you. They will come to your home when you need them and provide ongoing help both in managing symptoms and in teaching you what to expect tomorrow based on how your child is doing today. The hospice nurses and the physician in charge, usually your child's primary doctor but sometimes a hospice medical director, are available on call 24 hours a day to help you.

If the professionals who will help you at home are not hospice nurses or are inexperienced with children, and they are the only service available, you may have situations where you don't feel you are getting help fast enough, or you may not agree with the nurse's plan. You may need to establish with the doctor in charge a phone number that you can call to speak with her if you need to, at any time of day, to discuss these things.

Help from family and friends is even more crucial when your child is dying at home than it is when she's in the hospital. If you are going to be up at night caring for your child, you will need someone to help you during the day so you can sleep. Family and friends can cook special meals, bring pets and visitors, and create a warm, pleasant atmosphere without the institutional limits that come with a hospital. (Hospice services do have some volunteers to help with this as well.) And again remember that many people will be anxious to help. They too are grieving the coming loss of this child, and they are grieving for your grief. Allowing them to be useful helps them to cope with these feelings.

Many parents have fears about caring for their dying child at home. That is normal. They worry that a medical problem will arise for which they are not prepared. But if you know what to expect before the death, during the death, and afterward, you can prepare. We will discuss symptoms before death, and their management, later in the chapter. You should remember, though, that you can go back to the hospital if you need to: Your decision is not irreversible.

I've seen this happen several times. In one case, Charlene, a 5-year-old dying from advanced cancer that had spread throughout her abdomen and lungs, was doing well enough to play quietly with her brother. She was not eating or drinking much, and was getting more and more tired. Her parents were working with a hospice team and their primary medical team to decide where she would be when she died, and the parents were torn. Her father wanted her in the hospital because he was very comfortable with the doctors and nurses, and so was Charlene. He was afraid also of the bad memories Charlene's brother might have if Charlene died at home. Her mother had a gut feeling that home was the right place but dreaded being unable to handle her daughter's pain or fear. The family decided to keep her home, but the team stressed that if they changed their minds when Charlene began to get worse, they could reverse their decision. When that time came, they both felt that she would be better off in the hospital. She died there, peacefully in her mother's arms, with the medical team available. Her parents are at peace with all of their decisions.

When thinking about the time that your child is actually dying, it can be hard to imagine being without medical help. This is one of the most important reasons to involve a hospice team, because they will send someone to be with you if you wish. It is important that nobody panic when your child's bodily functions slow down. When this happens, when her breathing is stopping, caregivers may suddenly feel utterly inadequate, and want to call 911. This is a sensible response when there is hope for recovery. But in the case of an expected death at home, this is time to get ready to help your child to die comfortably, following instructions developed beforehand. (We will cover this fully in Step Y.)

The family of Carrie, a 6-year-old with progressive cancer, decided to keep their daughter at home after experimental treatment failed. Carrie was well enough to play quietly at the time, so naturally her parents were considering further therapy. A referral was made to the palliative care team, as she was suffering from abdominal and bone pain. The staff got her symptoms under control and remained available to the family as needed. This made all the difference, because, as is only natural, the family sometimes doubted their decision to keep her home. They decided against chemotherapy, which at this point could do little to prolong her life. With help from the hospice team and the primary medical team, Carrie died at home, surrounded by her family and pets.

An important consideration when deciding whether to keep your child home at this time is how ready your other children are to cope with it. Families become appropriately concerned about the trauma of children having a sibling die at home, and about their seeing unpleasant things as they happen. With help from the hospice, Child Life, child psychology, pastoral care, and/or social work staff, you can prepare your other children. There are real advantages to this for the children. They feel part of things. They tend to imagine things worse than reality, and preparation prevents this. One 7-year old, Jared, told the nurses that he was frightened of seeing his sister dying, because "when people die they look awful and have green stuff pouring out of their eyes and ears." The nurses reassured him that, though his sister might be very weak when she died, she would look fine—and in fact, his being there could help her to die peacefully. He understood then, and was at her side with the rest of the family when she took her last breath at home in their parents' bed.

There are good resources available to help you to think about preparing your other children (or close young cousins or friends) for this experience. Some are listed in Further Resources.

The Decisions Are Yours

In thinking about where your child will die, at home or in the hospital, you have to contemplate something that is utterly heartbreaking. And you have to think about how it will affect you and your other children in the future. The choice will depend on many things, the most important of these being your child's medical condition, the resources available to you, and your feelings about each option. Don't hesitate to ask for advice from the health care team, friends, and family. Feelings that you can't do this, that you can't decide, and that you can't get through it may surface. The best thing you can do for yourself is to turn these feelings around. Recognize that you are doing the hardest, most selfless, and most loving work a parent ever could do. Take credit for that.

STEP S: DEALING WITH YOUR CHILD'S PHYSICAL CHANGES

This section, as we noted in the introduction to the chapter, will be difficult to read. But we believe, based on what dozens of parents have told us, that it will be somewhat easier for you to deal with the physical changes your child will go through when she is dying if you have heard of them before, and know what to expect. When describing what you may see, this section becomes unavoidably rather clinical, and this may cause it to sound cold. This is not our intention. Our goal is to help you with difficult, but essential, information.

The process of dying will bring about significant changes in your child's physical appearance and function. You need to anticipate and prepare for these changes. They are a natural part of the dying process and most do not need to be treated. Some medical teams will be better than others at helping you to know what is coming. Keep asking the question, "What should we expect to see next?" Let your medical team know if something in particular worries you.

Loss of Appetite and Thirst

As your child's bodily functions slow down, her appetite will probably decrease. She will gradually want smaller portions, and probably more fluids than solid food. As we discussed in Step G, there is no pain associated with this loss of appetite. Your child will not "starve to death." Similarly, she will gradually lose thirst. Sometimes she may need ice chips to moisten her mouth. Petroleum jelly can also moisten her dry lips.

The decreased need for food and drink is a natural part of the process of dying. How soon or how rapidly it develops is different with each situation. You may see your child's appetite fluctuate up and down for many days. You and the medical team can work with the fluctuations by simply having soft, easy-to-eat foods and a cup of juice or water handy at the bedside for when she asks for them. You should not, however, try to force her to eat or drink.

This can be hard for parents. Eating and having a good appetite are strongly associated with health in our culture. In our cure-based medical systems, many dying patients have needlessly had feeding tubes inserted or intravenous lines hooked up, for many reasons. These include the difficulty in predicting whether a child will be cured, and the emotional issues surrounding food and drink. But as the body is shutting down, to artificially give fluids or calories can create more stress on it and cause diarrhea and fluid buildup.

Further, intravenous fluids may cause swelling, or may go to the lungs and cause trouble with breathing. In contrast, the naturally occurring slowdown in fluid intake seems to produce endorphins from the brain, leading to less pain. So work with the doctors to continuously reevaluate the need for any medically given calories or fluids. Ask each time, "How will this improve my child's comfort?"

Losing Bodily Functions

You should expect that your child will experience fatigue and weakness, and will probably progress to a time when she stays in bed or, if she's at home, on the couch most of the day. She will lose the ability to walk any significant distance, so you may need a wheelchair or stroller, even at home.

Later in the process of dying, she will probably lose the ability to care for herself when urinating or voiding. You may start with bedpans or a bedside commode, but ultimately you will probably use diapers to care for her. Some parents prefer to use catheters. Depending on how old your child is, she may find all this upsetting, as will you. Tell her that you and any other caregivers are happy to help in this way, and that even though diapers may cause initial embarrassment, they help keep her clean. Younger children can be just as embarrassed about this as adolescents; this is another time to use the psychosocial team to help you.

Weight Loss or Swelling

Most children who die after a long-term illness have lost a lot of weight by the time they are dying. You might need to be prepared for your child to develop a rather emaciated look. In contrast, the treatments for certain conditions frequently result in extreme swelling, especially around the eyes, the face and head, or the abdomen. This kind of swelling can also be the result of the disease itself, especially heart disease, kidney disease, or some cancers. If the disease is a cancer in the abdomen, there can be a great deal of swelling there, both from the tumor and from the way it causes the body to retain fluids. Family members and friends who have not seen your child for a while may find such changes startling and upsetting, so be sure to mention the changes to new visitors before they see her; you don't want them to upset her and themselves by an instinctive exclamation. If you've taken photographs, consider whether it would be helpful to show them to visitors beforehand.

As hard as it is to see your child like this, you can find comfort for each other. Bereaved parents have given us several suggestions about this. Most important is simply to reinforce the fact that you know how beautiful your child is. You can do this both verbally and through tangible signs. Ten-year-old Yamin had always been a handsome child, and now his parents would bring that up frequently—"How's my gorgeous boy today?" they'd ask, and he would grin. They also brought to the hospital his favorite blue T-shirt and a few others in that color. Similarly, the parents of 15-year-old Gerda brought bottles of her nail polish to the hospital and changed the colors every other day. They also kept her favorite baseball cap nearby, so she felt less self-conscious about her thinning hair.

The key is to remind yourself what you really know deep down: that your child is always beautiful, because it's the soul that creates human beauty. If you project this, your child will pick it up.

Breathing Problems

Your child may experience some changes in breathing patterns. This can be frightening for anyone present, and hopefully the medical team will have you prepared for this.

The extent of the problem will depend on your child's condition.

As part of the natural process of dying, her breathing may be slower and more shallow. This creates a natural buildup of carbon dioxide—which itself triggers the body's attempts at deeper breathing, though that may not be possible because of the primary disease. These attempts may look like labored breathing. But she is not suffering. Excess carbon dioxide in the blood adds to the sleepiness and blunting of alertness that is already occurring—a kind of natural anesthetic. There may also be increasing numbers of pauses between breaths, which can get longer right before death. This is natural and does not cause her any suffering.

Your child may have actual labored breathing, which means the breathing is difficult because of fluid buildup, pneumonia, or other disease-related problems. This is called *dyspnea*. There is medication than can ease it. Most likely, her doctor will prescribe morphine. It can be given through an I.V. if she has one, but there are forms of it that can be given by mouth, under the tongue (so that swallowing is not necessary), or rectally if need be. The labored breathing can usually be settled, but not always immediately prior to death. If it's causing her anxiety, other medications can be used to help alleviate the discomfort. Together these medications successfully relieve the sense of breathlessness, though they do not necessarily change the pattern of the breathing itself. There is a misconception that giving such medicine actually stops the breathing. It is true that medicines like morphine can slow the rate of breathing, but when used to treat discomfort or dyspnea, they are helping the child. If they are given when the dyspnea is at its worst, it might be that this is right before the child dies. It does not mean the medicine causes the death. The death that was about to happen occurred, with no relation to the medication.

Sometimes fluids in the mouth and throat create a sound that has been called the "death rattle." This is simply the result of air moving through fluid. The child is unaware of the sound, but it can be distressing for those who are with her if they are unprepared for it.

Other patterns you may see are irregular breathing rates, where the child seems to breathe rapidly at one time, then slowly the next. Or, there may be a period in which there is no breathing for a minute or so, followed by the breath returning (this is called an "apneic" period).

Other Changes

Depending on their medical condition, some children are at risk of seizure near the end of their life. If your child is dying at home, you'll want to ask the doctors whether you should have medicine on hand to prevent or treat this.

There may be some changes in skin color; as the circulation becomes slower there can be an uneven, mottled look to her skin. Her eyes may close only halfway.

It's possible that she'll have some bleeding. If so, talk to the doctors and hospice staff about what to do. Sometimes a medication can help this. Be sure to have dark-colored towels handy: Lighter towels show the blood more vividly and can be distressing to you and your family.

She might appear restless or agitated at times. It will help to talk to the medical or hospice staff: This does not necessarily mean she is in pain, but it can be hard for you to tell. So, you should feel free to ask the medical or hospice team for help with this. Their experience will help you to know if a sedating medicine will be useful.

Throughout all of these difficult changes, it will be helpful to constantly tell your child how much you love her, and that she is safe, even if you think she cannot hear you. Most of us who work in this field believe that even at this stage a dying person hears the voices of loved ones.

CHAPTER 8

FINDING PEACE

I wouldn't change a thing about how my son died.

Once you realize that your child is going to die, it is important for you to take care of your own future needs. For whatever reasons, you will outlive your child, for many years. You will never see the same happiness you had before this loss, but you can have a different happiness. You can find some peace, even joy, in the years ahead. There are things you can do now to help bring about these conditions later.

STEP T: TELLING YOUR CHILD'S STORY AND MAKING MEMORIES

Most parents delight in telling stories about their children. You have days, weeks, or years worth of memories, going back to before your child was even born. These memories are part of your child's unique story. You may find now that telling such stories, out loud or in writing, will help you to focus on good times and to stay strong during this ordeal.

While you are with your child, it's good to go over these tales when people visit. This can turn into a time of sharing memories, both good and bad, funny and melancholy. Your family and friends may remember things that you have forgotten, or haven't heard about. This can add to your own memories about your child.

Some parents fear they will lose the memory of their child as time goes by. I have found that many have solved that problem through the use of writing and photographs and/or videos. Some have written their child's story from beginning to end.

The parents of Jamie, a teenager who died from cystic fibrosis, made a special request of family and friends. In a Christmas letter that went out about a month after her son died, his mother, Belle, asked people to write down their special memories of him. People wrote all kinds of things. One aunt remembered how Jamie had cried when he lost his first tooth and didn't want to let the tooth fairy take it away. A family friend who had taken Jamie to his first baseball game wrote lovingly about the camaraderie they'd shared that day. The clinical staff wrote about how he had never failed to make them laugh with his funny antics. When she received these, Belle compiled them into a special album of memories and photographs. The whole family treasures this book. Another family received such a journal of memories and passed it among family and friends: Spontaneously, these people wrote their own memories on the blank pages. When the book came back, it was fuller and richer than it had been before.

I would recommend that you think about that ahead of time. Consider how dear your child's life and unique story have been to you. Organize the photographs of him (or delegate this task). Take more photos now. Write stories down. Tell these stories to the people around you—even the doctors and nurses. Home nurses and hospice nurses in particular love these stories. Tell them to your child during your times together, too; it can become a way to let him know how precious these times have been to you. It is often reassuring for the dying child to hear that these stories and memories will continue to be shared, and that he will not be forgotten after death.

You can take the lead in this regard on holidays, birthdays, and anniversaries. Place photos, awards, and other mementos in a prominent place at these times. One family I know lost their son Sean to cancer. Every Christmas they share a time of telling stories about Sean. They light a candle that sits by his photos and memorabilia.

STEP U: RECOGNIZING AND HONORING YOUR CHILD'S LIFE

When parents face the death of a child, they inevitably wonder in their agony why this has happened to their child and their family. You have probably felt that your child's life is being cut short, before he can make his mark on the world.

Perhaps when this occurs to you, it will help to think about the meaning your child's life has had already, about how he has affected the lives of those around him. You know how much he has meant to you; but you may be gratified to know what he has been to others as well. Share these thoughts with him: It can help a child to know that who he has been and what he has done is important. We have already reviewed some of the developmental tasks that children can accomplish, or jobs that they can do, to leave their mark (see Step L). It can also be amazing to list all the people whose lives have been touched in such a short time.

This can be true even with a very young child. If your child is dying while he's in the neonatal intensive care unit, you have had him for a very short time. But in that time, your family has probably learned a lot about the powerful love a little baby can bring out in people. Grandparents and aunts and uncles, brothers and sisters and cousins may all have had a chance to love this little person. They will remember that love and this will honor your child.

You, your child, and your family may have faced a long-term illness, with many treatments and much time spent in the hospital and clinic. Or maybe you've been in the intensive care situation for a short time—for example, after a car crash. Either way, you all faced it bravely, even if at times you became frustrated and angry. You may have heard a hundred times, "I don't know how you do it. Where do you get the strength?" You have probably wanted to answer that you have had no choice, that you did what you had to do. But your child's strength has probably been a source of pride for you, and a source of inspiration for the people, young and old, in his life. The adults who have gone through this with you are no doubt hoping that they will face the adversity in their lives with the simple grace that your child has shown.

If your ill child is school-aged or an adolescent, he may have learned some hard life lessons through this, such as who his friends really have been. My experience is that ill children seem older and wiser than their years. It may have been hard for you to observe, but again, it is wise to take pride in the strength, emotional growth, and resilience that your child has exhibited. There is no question that others have learned with and through him, and these are lessons that most of them will remember.

Remember to tell your child that you are proud of him. In the times when you are deeply sad, tuck that feeling of pride into your heart, and make it permanent. Memorize it.

How has your child been extraordinary? Has it been his delightful sense of humor that all the nurses notice? Has it been his funny infant smile? Perhaps it has been his playfulness, or his quiet, stoic demeanor. It may have been writings, or drawings, or special abilities or perceptive questions. Everyone knows that you would trade any of this in an instant to have him healthy again. But since this won't happen, take pride in what he has accomplished. *Your child will never be forgotten.*

STEP V: *Identifying and Removing Barriers to Peace of Mind*

As your child's death actually approaches, it becomes more and more important to set short periods of time aside and allow yourself to think and reflect. That may seem hard to do at a time of whirlwind emotions, but it is precisely because of those emotions that you need to do this thinking. It will help you achieve what peace of mind is possible, now and in the future. "Peace of mind" is not some impossible cliché. In the context of medical issues, it is a state in which regrets and conflicts are minimized. It is not some kind of Pollyanna cheerfulness; it will not mitigate your loss. But it will help you survive and move on with your life as your child would want you to do.

You can work toward this. You have probably been trying to do so, but there may be unresolved issues that keep entering your mind. Is now the time to deal with these issues? Are there things you need to talk through with someone, but have lacked the time or courage? If these involve medical concerns, it is extremely important to find the right person(s) and discuss them. You may need to be reminded that the medical decisions you have made for your child were the right ones, given the information you had at the time. It is normal to go back and forth on these things somewhat, but if this is happening to a disturbing extent, then you need to have another meeting with the medical team. You'll probably be experiencing some guilt feelings since the instinctive belief that you should have been able to make things better for your child can be strong, even as your mind knows that you've done all you could. The medical and/or hospice team can reassure you, and reinforce what your mind knows, so that you can come to terms with your emotions.

If the issues are not medical, the same principles apply. If there is an issue that has left you angry or hurt, you can help yourself by sorting out what those feelings are and where they come from. Perhaps you feel betrayed by friends who didn't call or visit enough, by family members who have blamed you for your child's illness or death, or by employers who refused to give you enough time off to care for your child. Talk to a trusted friend, and you can decide whether now is the time to bring this issue out. It may not be, but at least you have separated it out from the things that need your attention now. The very act of putting it aside can help you to achieve peace of mind at this important time.

The Question of an Autopsy

An issue that is important in terms of your future peace of mind, after your child has died, is whether you want an autopsy (also called postmortem examination) to be done. This can be a terribly hard thing to think about, and many parents have not done so. When asked about an autopsy, they have automatically declined. Sadly, some parents have later regretted that decision, as they tried to sort out specifically what caused their child's death.

This can happen because, although the overall cause of death is the illness or injury, it's possible that what has happened to your child medically is not completely clear. You may feel that an autopsy is pointless, since you cannot change the fact that your child is dying or has died. It may feel like a bad idea to do anything else to his body. But an autopsy can be for your benefit, as well as for that of the medical team. Even with all the tests that get done during treatment, in about a quarter of cases the autopsy finds things that were not expected. It can be very hard for parents struggling months later with questions like, "Was it his lungs?" "Did he have bleeding or infection?" Without an autopsy, they might not have answers to those questions. Try to think about whether you will have those sorts of questions later; you may want to involve your close family members in this determination. Remind yourself that having an autopsy will not hurt your child; he cannot suffer anymore. An autopsy is done carefully and respectfully. Incisions will not show at the funeral; it is still possible to have an open casket. You also have the option of a "limited autopsy," in which only the specified organs in question are examined. (Understand, however, that all you are looking for is the specific cause of death at this time. You are not trying to figure out whether he might have survived if he had been given a different treatment.)

An autopsy can also help people other than yourselves. When doctors perform autopsies, they frequently learn more about the disease that killed the patient, and can apply that knowledge to research into the disease. Ask yourselves whether you and your child would want to help other children in this way. If you are considering this, you can ask the doctors whether there is any information to be gained that would help such children. The medical team wants to help gain this information, but their primary goal is to help you to achieve peace of mind down the road. You may not realize this when they ask you. It is really hard for doctors to ask parents about autopsies. They may do so rather quickly and rigidly, out of their own discomfort. Do yourself a big favor and think about this ahead of time. Let your doctors know you have given it this thought.

There are some differences across the country in terms of regulations about autopsies. You will need to ask your medical team to explain to you what the local rules are, including whether there will be any charge for the autopsy (there usually is not, but on rare occasions there is). If you do choose to have an autopsy done, speak with your doctor about a plan for reviewing the results with you later, whenever you are ready.

The Question of Organ Donation

Some parents ask about donating their child's organs, which is an incredibly unselfish and beautiful gift to offer. The easiest way to handle this is to have as much planned as far in advance as possible: Your child's doctor and health care team will be able to assist you with these arrangements. But even when plans are made ahead of time, last-minute changes can be handled. You may decide, when the time comes, that you no longer wish to do this, and arrangements can be quickly canceled. Or, you may suddenly want to pursue organ donation as your child's death draws near. Some parents find that organ donation creates a living legacy, helping their child live on through others. Either decision is fine and is yours to make. Keep in mind, though, that your child's illness may make organ donation impossible (if, for example, your child has an infection of the blood or certain types of cancer). It is best to let your health care team handle the particulars about organ donation, and they should also be able to answer any questions you have about the process. In fact, even if you don't ask, you will probably be approached about the process by someone on the health care team, as this is required in most states.*

STEP W: *Thinking About the Funeral*

When your child dies, you will need to choose a funeral home. If you can think about it ahead of time, or ask someone to find out what your choices are, you will save yourself some effort later. Have someone in your support network ask directors of different funeral homes whether they have had experience with a family who has lost a child. The pastoral counselor or social worker from the medical or hospice team can be very helpful with this.

---

*You can find pertinent information on sites such as www.unos.org (this is the United Network for Organ Sharing) and www.shareyourlife.org.

A friend or family member can also help you prepare the clothing that your child will wear. You may have the outfit in mind. Your helper can get it cleaned if necessary, and make sure that it is ready for you.

Your child's friends, especially if they are teenagers, are probably feeling very helpless at this time. They may not get much help in dealing with their grief at losing a friend. It can be a comfort to both them and you if they can somehow be involved in the funeral or memorial service. They can prepare a reading and select a person from among them to read the piece, or they can select a special song. They may have some pictures from better times that they can use to create a collage. Talk with these children and their parents as time and your child's condition allow.

A group of teenagers was particularly helpful to the parents of a 16-year-old boy who died of a head injury. They assembled a wonderful photo collage on a poster, and it was used at the funeral, where several of Tommy's friends did readings. They spoke of what Tommy had meant to them and of important experiences they'd had together. This created a strong bond between them and Tommy's family, and indeed they continued to help the family down the road.

You should prepare yourself for the possibility that your child may present to you some ideas for his own funeral. Such a child is obviously very comfortable talking to his parents, and you should take comfort and pride in that. Be open to talking about it, and assure him that his wishes will be carried out. He may want to plan what to wear, the music, and the readings, for example. It is his way of finding meaning and having closure.

Your other children should be involved in funeral preparations as much as they like. Studies have shown that bereaved children are better able to deal with their grief when they are allowed to participate in planning, and to attend funerals of their loved ones. Depending on their age, they will ask questions about dying and what happens afterward. Talk to the Child Life practitioner or child psychology, pastoral care, and/or social services staff available to you to get some help in advance about what these questions might be, and how to answer them. (See Step I.) These professionals are a very good resource at this time; you will probably be glad you asked for this help.

STEP X: *Preparing the Other Children for Imminent Loss*

Your other children's lives have been disrupted, however much you've done to maintain their normal activities. Although it is nobody's fault, a tremendous emotional upheaval is taking place. As your ill child's death draws near, it becomes important to offer as much support as possible to your other children.

Just as it was important earlier to share information about their sibling's illness, it is important now to discuss his upcoming death. Use honest, direct, and simple language that children can understand. Give them the opportunity to be involved. Some siblings feel useful when they are allowed to stay with you as you tend to the dying child.

Let them do so. Reassure them again that nothing they said or did caused the illness.

Some common reactions you may observe in grieving siblings may be anger, problems in school, complaints of physical symptoms, fear/anxiety, regression to behavior they had engaged in at an earlier age, sadness, and withdrawing from activities. Such behaviors provide you as a family the opportunity to find out what questions the child may have, but may not know how to ask. For example, 4-year-old Ted became very withdrawn and quiet after his older sister had died. His mother told him in simple language what had happened to cause all the upset that he was witnessing. "How long will my people be sad?" he asked her. She was able to reassure him that, although they'd always have some sadness about losing his sister, their lives would become happy again soon.

Other children may cope with the situation by distancing themselves from their parents and their ill sibling. It may seem that they are doing all right, because they do not vocalize their concerns or act withdrawn. It can be helpful to remind such a child that you are available to talk if he would like to. While he will cope according to his age by taking time for himself, it is important for him to know that he has been given honest answers.

You may have a child who seems to be coping just beautifully, helping you in every way, and going on with life as if nothing is wrong. While that may feel like a relief, it can be cause for some concern. This "perfect sibling" may not be dealing with things at all. It would be wise to discuss this with the medical and hospice staff, and at a very minimum to have a conversation with him using guidance from the medical team. And have his physician and schoolteacher help you to evaluate how he does in the future as well.

Any person involved in your child's life, particularly his schoolteacher, should be told about his sibling's death and how he is coping with it. The classroom becomes a second home for the child, and may provide a safe place for him to express himself.

Use the medical team or the hospice bereavement specialist or social worker to help you with the children, as far in advance as you can manage. Their suggestions and support will be practical, and will include things that you and the rest of your loved ones can do together, so you don't feel like you are dealing with your child's reaction alone. In addition, if there is a sibling support group in your community, consider having your children participate.

This book cannot cover all the many differences in normal grieving seen in the different developmental levels of children of various ages. Some useful resources for dealing with your children's bereavement are listed in Further Resources.

STEP Y: DEALING WITH THE DEATH OF YOUR CHILD

In Step S, while discussing physical changes to prepare for and deal with, we talked about the medical things that happen as death approaches. Other changes will happen at the time of the death itself. Reading about this will be especially emotional for you, and you might not want to read this section for the first time if you are alone with your children. In fact, it might be a good idea to have a close friend or your spouse with you. But it's important that, at some point before your child dies, you do read it. Again, preparation makes it easier to be there for your child as the changes happen—and that, above all, is what you want to do.

It's tremendously important now to keep in mind all the work you have done for your child throughout his illness or injury episode. Self-doubt may reemerge as his death comes closer. Be kind to yourself. You have been doing the best you can in the most painful situation any parent can face.

It often helps to have a plan in place for when death is near. Who will you call to be with you (family, friends, clergy-person, hospice or home care nurse)? It is important to have the people with you that you can trust to help you. Who will you need to call afterward (hospice or home care nurse, physician, coroner, funeral home)? A plan is extremely important, because panic and anxiety are common at such a time. You will want to avoid having things done that are against your or your child's wishes.

Other questions to plan for with your team are these: Who will declare the child dead? (At the hospital, this will be the doctor on duty. At home, this will probably be the home care or hospice nurse.) Will there be an autopsy (see Step V)? Where will your child's body be taken after death and how will he be transported? If there is an autopsy, he will be taken first to the hospital's pathology morgue to have it done, and then to the funeral home. How will you let your family and friends know that your child has died? It is probably a good idea to ask a friend or family member to help make calls.

As your child dies, it is time to trust your instincts again. They will tell you to embrace your child, or hold his hand, or stroke his hair. You may want to play the music you have enjoyed together before, and bring in the people that you want present. Your child can hear you even if he is not responsive; tell him that you love him, and that you always will. Let him know that it is all right for him to leave you: that although you will miss him, you will be okay and the family will take care of each other. Remind him that he will never be forgotten, and that you have been lucky to have shared his life with him. Continue to do those things that you and your child, as well as your other children and family members present, find comforting. Some parents find it helpful to have some type of baptism, healing, or other prayer service. If you belong to a church or other religious organization, or if you would like the medical team spiritual counselor to help, this can be arranged at any hour of the day or night.

You should be able to do these things regardless of where you are, home or hospital. If it is a hospital setting, work with staff to relax any visiting rules ahead of time. They should be able to accommodate the people that you want to have with you. They can get rid of I.V. lines that are not needed for comfort medications, and they can minimize monitors, leaving only those that you want. Blood pressure and temperatures do not need to be checked, and people that you don't want in the room should not be there.

If you are home, you may want to have a member of the hospice or medical team with you as your child dies. This means you will need to anticipate when to call, and this in turn means *you need to know when the time of death is near.* This can be hard to tell, but there are some anticipatory signs, and the hospice team can teach you these in advance. Ask them or your doctor to tell you what to watch for; these things can vary depending on the illness, just as the earlier signs can. The most important thing to know is that the moment of death can be truly peaceful, and in my experience, it usually is. Parents who have held their children at the time of death tell us about how they felt them leave in a restful way, after their breathing gradually slowed and then stopped.

The most common anticipatory signs are these: The child has stopped drinking, and the amount of urination has slowed and nearly stopped. He has been sleepier, and may have stopped opening his eyes or talking. Often breathing becomes slower and less regular, and his heart rate can slow as well; however, some dying children actually breathe faster and have a faster-than-normal heartbeat. His skin can change to a darker, purplish color where it is touching the bed and blankets, because the circulation is slowing. There will be some blue color at the fingers, toes, and lips, and this will spread to the rest of his skin, which begins to feel cool especially at his hands and feet.

As we discussed in Step S, his breathing may appear more labored, and you may hear some fluids moving in his throat, which sounds like a rattling. At times there can be seizures, too (this is more likely with some conditions than others).

The doctors and hospice team will probably have talked to you earlier about using medicines to prevent this.

Most often, breathing will just slow to a peaceful stop, and the heart will stop shortly after that. Sometimes, though, if there were seizures, it may not feel peaceful to you. Your child may lose control of his bodily functions. His pupils stay one size (they become "fixed"), and his eyes may stay open. Though this may be jarring to you, it isn't to him. He doesn't know what his body is doing at this stage. Once the breathing has ended, his heart will stop within a few seconds to minutes, and he will die.

If your child is dying in the hospital, the process can also be peaceful and comfortable, but it is different in some ways. His heart may stop with the ventilator still going. In this case the changes just described will still happen, except that the breathing rate, controlled by the machine, does not change. If the ventilator is being turned off, then the breathing tube is either taken out or kept in, and you can decide with the team which way would be best. Either way, your child can lie in bed or in your arms, and his heart will likely stop within minutes. The changes described above will take place during this time. If the ventilator has been turned off, ask the doctors to explain how medicines are used to keep him comfortable until he dies. These medicines *do not* stop the heart or breathing—the medical condition does this. The medicines simply get rid of any pain.

Perhaps this seems impossible for you to do. But it isn't. The love you have for your child will carry you through, knowing that you are doing not what you so desperately wish you could do, but all you can do to make his dying comfortable. You are giving him more than many dying people will ever have.

A mother and father I watched rage against the disease that was taking the life of their baby made peace with the fact that little Joy would die within a few days. When she was clearly too sick to survive, they decided with the doctor to turn off the ventilator. They held her in their arms and sang to her until her last breath. She died looking totally peaceful and beautiful, and her parents said they were "kissing her on her way to heaven."

Sometimes, you are not able to be present at the moment your child dies. This moment is not always predictable, especially for children, since their bodies are so young and otherwise strong. Because of that, some parents hold an exhausting vigil over days to weeks. But you'll have to sleep, and your child may die during that time. Another possibility is that you and the medical team were preparing for a slow worsening, and instead a quick change in your child's condition resulted in his death much sooner than you expected. If you are not present, for this or any other reason, you may feel guilty. Remember that you cannot control everything: If this happens, be kind to yourself and cherish the good things you did for your child while he was living, and while he was dying. You may not be able to entirely avoid regretting what was left undone, but balance that by knowing what a good job you did, and how much you *did* get done. Many people believe that the dying choose the moment at which they let go. It may be that your child needed to wait until you left in order to be able to slip away. If this is how it happens, there is still the time to be with your child, to hold him, and to say good-bye.

Ask for all the help you need, ask the questions you need to, and you will be able to help your child to a peaceful death.

Well done.

Epilogue

I could have used help with the grieving part. I had to find my own way.

What? No Step Z? Where is Step Z?

There it is, that feeling that the book did not end right. Your gut has known for a long time that something is not right: It's a familiar feeling. It comes with the need to make everything the way it should be.

So do you feel you got it right for your child and your family? You have been through the hardest thing a person ever faces, and you deserve to take some credit for that. Still it is natural for a parent to feel that the world is no longer right. You will probably find that you can't shake that feeling for awhile, at least until you have found your new normal.

For now, the new normal includes grieving.

Here we offer a little more information that will be helpful to you, things about what happens right after the death, and some words about bereavement. Because it is beyond the scope of this book to cover the topic completely, other resources are listed at the end of the book.

After the Death

After your child dies, you may stay with her as long as you like. If you are in the hospital, it will feel very hard to leave. If at home, it will be hard to see her taken away. Most often, the funeral home that you have chosen will come to do this.

If you have decided to have an autopsy done, or to donate your child's organs, this will happen at the hospital. After that, the funeral home staff will take your child to their building. There they work with you to find out what your funeral plans are, and they will help you to make the decisions that you need to make, including deciding between cremation and burial. It will help if you have thought about these things ahead of time. (See Step W.) You have the opportunity to spend more time with your child's body at the funeral home. You can place loved items with the child in the casket, leaving them there just for the wake, or for always.

If and how a wake is held, and how the funeral will be conducted, depend on your culture and belief system. This is all about how to memorialize your child, which is a very individual thing. The Further Reading section lists a very helpful book about this, entitled *To Comfort and to Honor: A Guide to Personalizing Rituals for the Passing of a Loved One,* by Jeanne McIntee. Sometimes parents initially feel that they don't want to have a wake, that it will be too difficult, and then change their minds, often finding themselves gratified by how many people were there to honor and remember their child.

The important thing to keep in mind is that this is your time to complete the process in the way that works best for you and your family. Many people will have suggestions or "shoulds" to offer, but this is not the time to give in to someone else's wishes unless they match your own. This is especially the case if your child has helped to plan her own funeral; honoring her desires may mean saying no to other people.

Going Through the First Year of Grieving

Grieving involves various stages and many emotions, and a complete discussion of these things is beyond our scope here. We'll cover some of the basics, however.

Because there is so much to do in the first few hours and days after your child's death (chiefly preparing for the funeral), things may feel blurred and you may feel numb. Being surrounded by family and friends can help you to get through these days. Most often there are calls and visits for days and weeks right after that, and hopefully you can let people know what you need, and how they can help you.

In the weeks that follow, the time will come when your family and friends start getting back to their routine. This might happen before you have established *your* new routine, though. You might want to consider working with a grief counselor for yourselves and your other children to help you make this difficult transition.

Grieving is hard work; it can make you feel tired even if you haven't been physically active. Grief tends to have a roller-coaster effect: Feelings like sadness, anger, loneliness, fear, and/or guilt sometimes come in waves when you least expect them. And the unpredictability of these strong emotions can make them feel out of your control. That's where support from family, friends, and community can be helpful.

The months ahead are especially hard because of all the "firsts." There is the first Mother's Day, the first Father's Day, the first time your child's birthday comes around, the first winter holidays, and then the first anniversary of the death itself. When each of these days arrives, remember that different parents in your situation choose to handle these days differently, depending on what is right for them. You may want to do what you've always done on these days, or you may want to develop another tradition in which to remember your loved one who died. The only way for others to know what you prefer is if you let them know. Perhaps those closest to you can help you figure out what you want to do.

Your family and friends may expect you to be back to normal after the first year, or even sooner. While you will probably be back in the world, you won't be back to "normal." You will be finding your way to a new normal. Instead of resenting these people, let them know how you are working to honor your child's memory, and how they might best help you to do that.

There are many support groups available in most communities for people who have suffered the death of a child. Some groups, like Compassionate Friends, offer support for those parents who have experienced the death of a child from any cause. Others target a specific cause of death, like cancer. You can call one of these organizations to find a contact person to direct you to the right place. You can also call your local hospice to find out about supportive resources available in your community. The thought of attending a support group may seem frightening to you, but give it a try. In such an environment, you will be given a chance to interact with people whose situations may be similar enough to yours that they can understand some of your feelings. Supporting yourself and those around you will help you with your grief. There are also support groups on the Internet.

You and your spouse may mourn differently, and may not be able to support each other at each moment of your grieving. Predictably, this tends to play out around gender lines: Women are more likely to let their feelings out, and men to hold theirs in. But even if your feelings are completely compatible, you each may find additional comfort in different sources of support. Allow yourself both your common and your separate mourning. Things that you both might expect to see and experience include sadness, depression, loss of appetite and energy, and difficulty sleeping. These are more common in the first six to nine months after your child's death, but there is no right amount of time to grieve.

One of the wonderful things about being a parent is your pride in your child. You will miss the many things she did that you felt proud of during her life: bringing home a great report card, hitting a home run or scoring a goal, drawing a beautiful picture, being kind to others, being courageous, or being a lot like you. Now you can be proud of what she was to you and to others while she was alive, and of the memories that you shared.

But there is something else. As hard as this experience has been on you and your family, and as hard as you have worked getting through it, be proud of yourself as a parent. Your child would certainly be proud of you. And she probably still is.

Further Resources

We could not possibly list all of the excellent books and other resources available to help you. Below we list some Web sites that offer resources:

For a list of books that help children to deal with death, visit:
www.compassionbooks.com

The Candlelighters Childhood
Cancer Foundation
P.O. Box 498
Kensington, MD 20895-0498
(800) 366-2223
www.candlelighters.org

Children's Hospice International
901 North Pitt Street, Suite 230
Alexandria, VA 22314
(800) 2-4-CHILD or
(703) 684-0330
www.chionline.org

**Children's International Project on
Palliative/Hospice Services (ChIPPS),
National Hospice and Palliative Care Organization**
1700 Diagonal Road, Suite 300
Alexandria, VA 22314
www.nhpco.org

The Compassionate Friends, Inc.
P.O. Box 3696
Oak Brook, IL 60522-3696
(877) 969-0010
www.compassionatefriends.org

Growth House, Inc.
Excellent source for publications and
links regarding end-of-life care
(415) 255-9045
www.growthhouse.org

FURTHER READING

For Adults Reading About the Death of Children

Arnold, Joan Hagan, and Gemma, Penelope Buschman. *A Child Dies: A Portrait of Family Grief.* The Charles Press, Philadelphia, 1994. This book will be helpful to grieving families, as it sorts through the grief reactions associated with the loss of an infant, child, or adolescent. It is especially useful for those looking to find some meaning in loss.

Davies, Betty. *Shadows in the Sun: The Experiences of Sibling Bereavement in Childhood.* Brunner/Mazel, Philadelphia, 1999. This book includes practical guidance for both parents and professionals trying to help children grieving the death of a sibling. The early and long-term issues are covered in a comprehensive and quite helpful fashion, using research findings and the family situation of each particular child.

DeYmaz, Linda. *Mommy, Please Don't Cry.* Multnomah Books, Sisters, Oregon, 1996. This book is written in the style of the child in heaven as the narrator, describing the wonders of heaven to the bereaved mother. It has a comforting style; it is clearly for the Christian reader as the child does describe Jesus.

Grollman, Earl. *Talking About Death: A Dialogue Between Parent and Child.* Beacon Press, Boston, 1990. This is a sensitive, comprehensive review of talking with children about the death of loved ones. There are modeled conversations and age-appropriate guidelines as well as a very complete list of resources.

Kroen, William C. *Helping Children Cope with the Loss of a Loved One: A Guide for Grownups.* Free Spirit Publishing, Minneapolis, 1996. In this book, Dr. Kroen offers sound and clearly written advice to adults helping a child cope with death. He includes stories of real children and their families, and explains how children from infancy to age 18 think about and react to death. He also gives suggestions for how to respond to children at these different ages and developmental levels, with very specific strategies.

Levand, Elizabeth, and Ilse, Sherokee. *Remembering with Love: Messages of Hope for the First Year of Grieving and Beyond.* Fairview Press, Minneapolis, 1995. This is a compassionately written book for the lonely and painful days of grief. There are short essays written by people who have experienced this grief and have come through it. It delivers an uplifting message while also helping the reader to know that their many difficult emotions are normal.

Lynn, Joanne. *Handbook for Mortals: Guidance for People Facing Serious Illness.* Oxford University Press, New York, 1999. While this book is largely for adults facing their own serious illness, there is a single chapter covering the death of children.

McIntee, Jeanne. *To Comfort and to Honor: A Guide to Personalizing Rituals for the Passing of a Loved One.* Augsburg Fortress, Minneapolis, 1998. This book was written by a woman who lost her son to cancer. It discusses the planning of funeral services and other memorials in a way that includes the personal characteristics and desires of the one who died. It is not specific to any one faith.

Rich Wheeler, Sarah, and Pike, Margaret M. *Goodbye My Child.* The Centering Corporation, Omaha, Nebraska, 1992. This book deals with the death of children of all ages and includes information on organ donation, autopsy, and funeral arrangements. It also deals well with the grief experienced by grandparents, brothers and sisters, and friends.

Rosof, Barbara. *The Worst Loss: How Families Heal from the Death of a Child.* Henry Holt and Company, New York, 1994. This book describes the process of grieving that adults go through, and also describes the grief process of children.

Rothman, Juliet. *The Bereaved Parents' Survival Guide.* Continuum Publishing Group, New York, 1997. This book was written by a grief counselor who is herself a bereaved parent, and gently guides parents through an explanation of the stages of grieving. It contains suggestions for difficult but practical topics such as what to do with the child's belongings, and where and how to reach out for help.

Schaefer, Dan, and Lyons, Christine. *How Do We Tell the Children? A Step-by-Step Guide for Helping Children Two to Teen Cope When Someone Dies.* Newmarket Press, New York, 1993. This book offers practical and clearly written advice for adults who must talk to children of all ages about death. This is done in the context of the different developmental ages of children.

Wagner, Shelly. *The Andrew Poems.* Texas Tech University Press, Lubbock, 1994. These are poems written by the mother of a little boy who drowned. Her eloquent expressions of grief but also of the joy of her parenting bring comfort and a message to bereaved parents that they are not alone in their pain.

Zeitlin, Steve, and Harlow, Ilana. *Giving a Voice to Sorrow: Personal Responses to Death and Mourning.* Perigee Press, New York, 2001. While this book is not solely about children, it contains very personal and powerful examples involving parents and children. In particular, the story is told of a girl of six who deals with her own death in a way that is very meaningful to her parents.

For Adolescents Facing the Death of a Loved One

Fitzgerald, Helen. *The Grieving Teen: A Guide for Teenagers and Their Friends.* Fireside, New York, 2000. This book can be used by both the teen and his or her parents; the many aspects of grief from different sources are discussed.

Gravelle, Karen, and Haskings, Charles. *Teenagers Face to Face with Bereavement.* Messner, New York, 1989. Seventeen teenagers and young adults describe in their own words their experience with bereavement and list their suggestions for other teens going through such loss.

Grollman, Earl. *Straight Talk About Death for Teenagers: How to Cope with Losing Someone You Love.* Beacon Press, Boston, 1993. This is a text geared for teenagers, written in a straightforward yet sensitive manner.

For Younger Children

Romain, Trevor. *What on Earth Do You Do When Someone Dies?* Free Spirit Publishing, Minneapolis, 1999. The author talks to children on their own level about what they may be feeling after the loss of a loved one. He speaks from his own experience and makes very practical suggestions right to the child.

Varley, Susan. *Badger's Parting Gifts*. Lothrop, Lee, and Shepard, New York, 1984. This is a children's storybook, telling the story of the death of Badger, who was everyone's friend. His woodland friends grieve, but go on to memorialize their friend.

For All Ages

Bills, Taylor, Schweibert, Pat, and DeKleyen, Chuck. *Tear Soup*. Perinatal Loss, Portland, 1999. This is a beautifully illustrated storybook that will be comforting to both adults and children. It tells the story of "Grandy," who has suffered a loss, and so begins to make tear soup. This reflects her individual process of healing, which includes the support of people and pets in her life.

Hanson, Warren. *The Next Place*. Walden House Press, Minneapolis, 1997. This is a beautifully illustrated and inspirational book describing the feelings, colors, and timelessness of "the next place." There is an uplifting sense of wonder, contentment, serenity, and utter acceptance and anticipation as the writer describes the journey from here to there.

For Parents in the Midst of Dealing with Their Seriously Ill Child

Burd, Larry. *Endings*. University of North Dakota School of Medicine, Grand Forks, 2001. This booklet raises the questions parents need to think about if their child has a terminal illness. This is not a place to find the answers, but rather to find the questions that parents need to ask medical staff in terms of making decisions and preparing for the death of their child.

Crawford, Bonnie, and Lazar, Linda. *In My World: A Journal for Young People Facing Life-Threatening Illness.* The Centering Corporation, Omaha, Nebraska, 2001. This is a "fill in the blank" type of book for adolescents who are facing life-threatening illness. It lets them fill the blanks about things like "all about me, the things I have done, if my future were left up to me to plan," and so on. Parents report that their children found it valuable, and that they as parents value its content years later, as well as "in the moment."

Moldow, D. Gay, and Martinson, Ida. *Home Care for Seriously Ill Children: A Manual for Parents.* Children's Hospice International, Alexandria, Virginia, 1991. This booklet concentrates on the medical issues around death and dying, and provides more detail about handling them. It is written in an understandable fashion, and will be a useful tool for parents to use to feel as though they asked their medical team all the necessary questions.

ACKNOWLEDGMENTS

I am very grateful to my colleagues who were willing to review this work and make suggestions:

There were colleagues who work with dying children. They are Drs. Jeanne Lewandowski, Suzanne Toce, Sarah Friebert, Joanne Wolfe, Kate Faulkner, Chris Hubble, and Dennis Pacl. Thank you for giving me the benefit of your experience and wisdom.

There were staff who work every day with dying children and their families. They are Cynthia Troy, Peggy Tuthill, Jody Chrastek, and Kelly Higgenbotham.

There were parents who went through the death of their own children. They are Karen O'Malley, Steve Steinmetz, Kelly Beaudot, Becky Wooten, Lynne Rief, Julie Macedo, Kathleen Bula, John and Karen Osen, Gail Lindekugel, and Honna Hodder. Thank you for reading something that would bring back memories of very hard days. You honor your children's memories as you help others by making this book better.

There were parents whose children went through very difficult treatment for medical illness, and are surviving. They are Pat Konkler, Lisa Baumbach, Nancy Keene, Janice Post-White, and Denny Lorentz. Thank you for helping me to understand what a parent needs when thinking about the possibility of their child dying.

Special thanks to Jan Watterson and Karen Lindsey, who helped me to write the words in a more gentle and kind way.

Thanks to the many colleagues who helped and encouraged me over the years and taught me their special skills. They include Sarah Friebert, Bruce Himelstein, David Freyer, Dan Tobin, Mary Kay Tyler, Jack Priest, Drew Ozolins, Bill Woods, John Kersey, Paul Orchard, Peggy Tuthill, Marion McNurlen, and Laura Matz. I also express my thanks to my dear colleagues in the Project on Death in America, with special thanks to Kathleen Foley.

Thanks go also to the people that I work with every day, that teach me how to work well with seriously ill, injured, or dying children and their families. It is a privilege to work with such compassionate people.

And to Roger, David, and Kelly, my extraordinary husband and children, who patiently wait for me. Your love and support is the wind in my sails.

There were and are the children. These are words that are from deep in my heart and are hard to get right. Thank you for touching my heart when you laughed, talked, smiled, cried, cursed, joked, played tricks, squirted me with syringes, and held my hand. I hope I helped you. I know you helped me.

Joanne Hilden

Special thanks to Fred Malphurs, Linda Weiss, Joe Engelhardt, Paula Hemmings, Paul Brenner, Don Schumacher, Vicki Weisfeld, Karen Kaplan, Myra Christopher, Kathy Foley, Ira Byock, Mary Anne Boe, Toni Stanton, Sharon VanDerWerken, Sherri Roff, David Becker, and Robert Spall for supporting this work. Special thanks to Richard and Beth Liebich and The Charitable Leadership

Foundation for having the vision and courage to fund the development of the PAICC program.

Daniel Tobin

We are very grateful to our agent, Jill Kneerim, and to Marnie Cochran of Perseus Publishing for her invaluable support and help.

Together we wish to thank Karen Lindsey for the wonderful experience and the privilege of writing with her.

Joanne Hilden and Daniel Tobin

Index

About The Children's
Hospital at The Cleveland Clinic

The Children's Hospital at The Cleveland Clinic is a 117-bed, acute-care pediatric hospital providing a homelike setting for young patients and their parents. The facility offers beds for medical/surgical, neonatal, child, and young adult intensive care, and is equipped with the latest medical technology, including a computerized epilepsy monitoring unit. The hospital is part of The Cleveland Clinic Foundation, a private, not-for-profit group practice based in Cleveland, Ohio. The Cleveland Clinic Children's Hospital for Rehabilitation is a 52-bed post-acute care unit augmenting the care received at the main hospital. Both are places for truly state-of-the-art therapy, where a child and family feel welcome and cared about.

Proceeds to Drs. Hilden and Tobin from this book are being donated to the care of children with advanced illness in Dr. Hilden's practice at The Children's Hospital at The Cleveland Clinic. This will help in the development of pediatric palliative care, and in the development of the Pediatric Advanced Illness Care Coordination (PAICC) program. For more information on the PAICC program, visit the Web site www.coordinatedcare.net (see PAICC listed in "provider" section under "activities").

About the Life Institute

Shelter from the Storm is a Life Institute book. The Life Institute is a nonprofit educational organization that works in collaboration with the VA Healthcare Network of Upstate New York. The Institute works to develop and implement programs in end-of-life care as well as wellness in aging. For more information about the Life Institute, write to:

**The Life Institute/VA Healthcare Network
of Upstate New York at Albany**
113 Holland Avenue (111t)
Albany, New York, 12208
or visit this Web site: www.coordinatedcare.net